Propellerhead
Reason TIPS AND TRICKS
5

Hollin Jones

PC Publishing

PC Publishing
Keeper's House
Merton
Thetford
Norfolk IP25 6QH
UK

Tel +44 (0)1953 889900
email info@pc-publishing.com
website http://www.pc-publishing.com

First published 2011

ISBN 13: 978 190600520 7

British Library Cataloguing in Publication Data
A catalogue record for this book is available from the British Library

Printed and bound in Great Britain by Jellyfish Solutions, Hants

Contents

Preface

For a long time, sequencing music on computers was predominantly the domain of people who had enough technical knowledge to understand the intricacies of their software. The need to make sequencers user-friendly was not highest on the list of manufactuter's priorities. For beginners or those with an intermediate level of technical skill, hardware was usually the best way to build a recording setup. Tape machines, drum machines, keyboard workstations and hardware samplers were the order of the day.

As with so many aspects of modern life, the computer quickly and decisively took over in the mid to late 1990s. As computers got more powerful and less expensive, owning and running a computer-based studio became a realistic goal for anyone interested in making music. As this happened, software manufacturers began to realise the potential that this new market offered them. When Propellerhead Software released Reason, it revolutionised the way we thought about sequencers. Based on the idea of a real rack of instruments, Reason just made sense and has become used and loved by a huge number of musicians and producers worldwide.

Reason's main strength is that it is as simple or complex as you want to make it. Beginners can be making music within ten minutes of having installed it. Seasoned users can get much more out of it than you'd guess at first glance. And it is for all Reason users that this book has been written. Every piece of software has hidden tricks, timesaving shortcuts and surprising features, and Reason is no exception. From its inception right up to the latest version 5 it's seen some major additions, new instruments and effects and workflow improvements that make it a great tool for musicians of all levels. Each instrument and effect is covered, as well as general working methods, workflow tips and advice on using computers for music production. It isn't an exhaustive list of every feature of every module, but rather a guide to using Reason in real-world situations. Only by using the program can you uncover its hidden depths, and this book provides useful insider tips that will help you be more creative, work faster and work smarter with Reason.

Reason is cross-platform, and so almost all tips apply to both Windows and Mac versions. Where there are differences, they are clearly marked. Whether you read the book cover to cover or just when you need to know more about a specific part of working with Reason, you're sure to learn something new that makes your Reason experience even better.

Setting up

Before you start

Making music is one of the most power-intensive things a computer can be asked to do. As CPU speeds go up, so do our expectations of what we should be able to do with our machines. Luckily, Reason's system requirements are considerably lower than those of many other sequencers. This is partly because it is self-contained, and because of that the programmers can fine tune it for maximum performance, knowing it won't have to deal with external plugins or third-party effects. But even though the minimum system requirements are relatively low, it's still highly recommended to get a powerful computer, preferably built specially for working with audio. An off-the-shelf PC might be OK but you'll find it may struggle with more intensive music projects. Here are some factors to consider when choosing a computer for audio work:

- Processor speed
- Hard drive size
- RAM capacity
- Expansion options
- Fan noise

Whilst most new PCs would meet the minimum system requirements for Reason, there are a number of arguments for buying one with a better specification.

- The faster the CPU, the more effects and instruments you can run. Most computers now use dual core CPUs or have four or even eight processors.
- A larger hard drive can store more data and helps modern operating systems to run more smoothly.
- More RAM means better sample playback, and generally helps a computer to run more efficiently and multitask.
- PCI and drive slots as well as USB and FireWire ports allow more flexibility to use audio and MIDI interfaces and add external hard drives
- A quieter computer is less likely to interfere with live recordings in other software such as Cubase or get in the way of monitoring and mixing.

Mac or PC

This is a long-running debate with staunch supporters on either side, but the sensible view is that both have their strengths and weaknesses. Increasingly for musicians your choice of platform is determined by your preferred sequencer. Logic, for example, is Mac only. SONAR by contrast is PC only. Reason, happily, runs on either, and the feature set on both platforms is identical. Since Apple moved its entire range to Intel processors, Intel-based Macs are capable of booting Windows natively or using virtualization software like Parallels, provided you have a Windows license. Though Macs are still often more expensive than PCs the relative difference has decreased sharply for machines of equivalent specification.

A quick comparison of Macs and PCs

The MacBook as shown in Figure 1.1 represents a surprisingly cheap and powerful entry-level Mac. Mac OSX tends to be very stable, and all Macs now have

Figure 1.1
Apple's MacBook is a low-cost but powerful entry-level system for running music applications.

Figure 1.2
The Mac Mini is a low-cost way to own a relatively powerful Mac.

Figure 1.3
PCs can be built to order from various components. More choice, but to avoid pitfalls, use a pro audio PC specialist.

at least a dual core processor. When you buy a Mac you know that it has been built to a specification set by Apple, and so hardware / software conflicts are rare. Peripherals often run without any additional drivers, and as an aside, Macs look good too!

Windows PCs are generally cheaper to buy, and building or buying one made of components you specify yourself is fairly straightforward. PC shops are found in every town, and though it will run on versions of Windows as far back as XP, Windows 7 will offer the best user experi-

ence thanks to its more modern design and underlying technology. A PC is more at the mercy of the drivers written for its components to allow them to talk to each other. A bad driver can mean hours spent on a helpline. Troubleshooting Windows can require a lot of technical knowledge, and it is prone to viruses, unlike the Mac.

A lot of people stick with what they know, and ultimately it's personal preference that will dictate your choice of platform. Luckily, Reason works well on both.

Installing Reason

On the Mac

Installation is fairly straightforward and everything now comes on a single DVD. On inserting the DVD you will see a simple window prompting you to drag the Reason folder to your Applications folder. After you have done this, go to the folder you just dragged into the Applications folder and double click the Reason application to open it. You will be prompted for your Administrator password, which is probably your regular password that you use for every install. The Reason installer will then copy the two sound banks

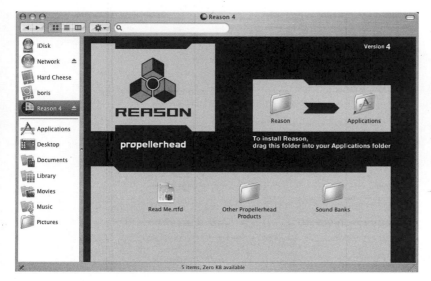

from the DVD to the Reason application folder. You must let it copy these to complete the installation. They use just over 2.6GB of space collectively which isn't much in this day and age. In theory you can drag this folder to any location but it's best to keep it in the Applications folder.

On the PC

Windows XP, Vista and WIndows 7 will probably autorun the Reason installer. If not, go to the start menu and select Run, then type d:/ or whatever the name of your optical drive is. Alternatively, click on My Computer > Program Disc and the installer will start. It's a good idea to quit all other running programs before starting the installer.

Info

Keep your operating system up to date with regular software updates. Unlike some sequencers, Reason takes OS updates in its stride, and doesn't tend to experience problems or glitches with incremental system changes.

Info

It helps to be logged in as an Administrator when installing. However, under Mac OSX, Windows XP, Windows Vista or WIndows 7 on your own computer, your regular account will probably be an admin account anyway.

Info

Any recent Mac will be running OSX. Reason 5 is a Universal Binary which means it will run happily on either an older PowerPC based Mac like a G4 or G5, or a more recent Intel-based Mac. It also runs well on OS X 10.4, 10.5 or 10.6.

Figure 1.4
Installing Reason on Mac OS X.

Figure 1.5
The installation procedure is very easy on both platforms.

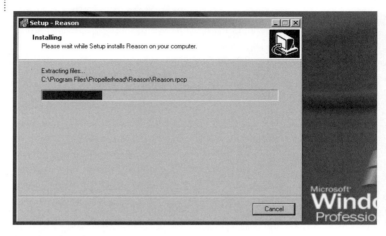

Location, location

Just like with Mac OS X, when installing Reason on Windows you have to install the sound banks by default. The installer will zip you through the process and provided you have adequate disk space there's nothing really to go wrong. Upon launching the program for the first time, the installer will copy the sound banks and you will be prompted for your license number.

Figure 1.6
Reason copies the Sound Banks during the installation process. It's sensible to keep them in the Reason folder.

Preferences

Reason's preferences determine how it interacts with your system and what settings it should use. They also let you tweak Reason for specific purposes and systems. The most important are the audio and MIDI settings, as they control how Reason receives and transmits all its data. Here is a look how best to set the preferences.

General

This, unsurprisingly, contains general settings for Reason's operation. The Appearance settings are a matter of personal choice, whether you want cables to animate and tooltips to appear. These are usually best left switched on. The Automation Cleanup control governs how much Reason "smooths out" the automation that you draw in the sequencer. Set low you can keep very precise settings though things can get fiddly. Set high, you get smoother, cleaner transitions.

The default song option lets you specify what Reason should do when you boot it up each time. By default it opens an empty rack, a blank canvas for you to start with. Selecting Built In opens the standard Reason demo song – which is a bit pointless to have open every time you start it up. The most useful option here is to select Custom, and use the file browser button to navigate to a project file. Let's say you always or more often than not work with the same kind of setup. A typical example of this might be a mixer, some reverbs and compressors, a piano and some drums and a bass loaded into various modules. Rather than having to manually add these each time, create a template song with all the modules set up but no MIDI recorded, and save it as a file called something like basictemplate.rns. If you set Reason to open this file on startup you'll save time setting up a new rack every session.

The CPU usage limit menu tells Reason at what point it should stop demanding more power from your processor. On a slower machine you may want to impose a limit, especially if you are running other software alongside Reason, so that it doesn't drain the system too much. Limiting it to 80% of the CPU would ensure it left some capacity for the other programs. In reality though, Reason is much kinder to processors than many other sequencers. Even on a moderately powered machine you will be able to switch this setting to No

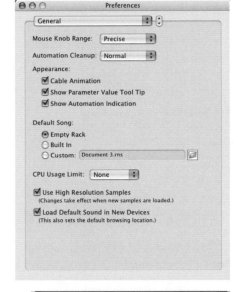

Figure 1.7
Specify a template song to load up when you start Reason.

Figure 1.8
Making template files read-only.

Info

Reason may periodically ask you to insert the program DVD for verification. It does this if it detects major changes in hardware or software configurations. Keep them to hand, and don't lose them.

Info

Remember, if using a template song, to save it as a new file name rather than just pressing save, or you'll save over your template.

Info

A good way to avoid accidental overwriting of template files is to make the templates read-only, preventing saving. On the Mac, use Get Info for a file and change its Ownership and Permissions to Read Only. On a PC control + click or right click the file, select Properties and change its attributes to Read-Only.

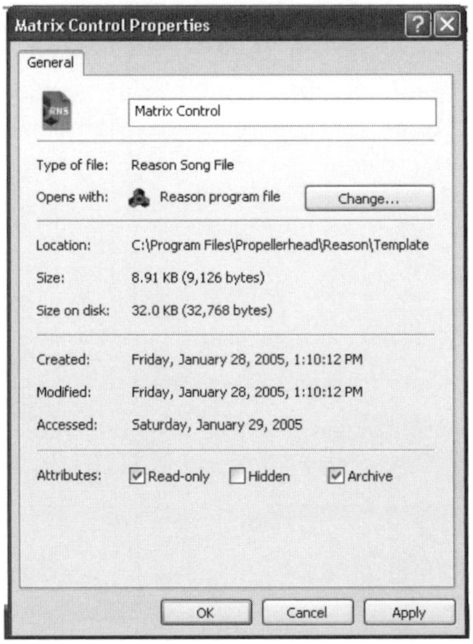

Figure 1.9
On most modern machines you can leave the CPU limiter effectively off.

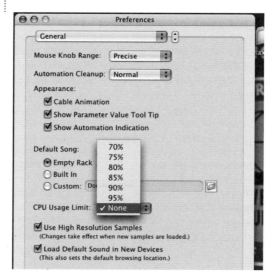

Limit and not notice any adverse effects until projects get very large. As all processing is done in-house, (inside Reason) the programmers have been able to optimize it for maximum CPU efficiency. On a modern machine you can leave the High Resolution Samples option switched on as well, as it's unlikely to trouble your computer. Current Dual and Quad Core processors have huge power when it comes to running Reason.

Audio

This is where you tell Reason which device to use to transmit and receive sound. The Master Tune control will alter the main tuning setting for the whole program. In practice you'll almost certainly never need to use this. The great thing about computer sequencers is that you can be sure they're always in tune. The only reason to use this would be in a situation where you had to

Figure 1.10
Choosing a sound output device.

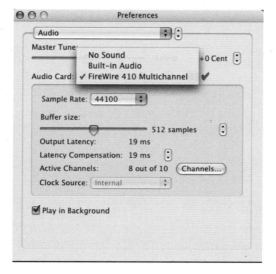

Tip

If you're just getting started and can't get any sound output, check that the program is set to use your sound card and isn't set to No Sound. Also check that your card drivers are up to date and that the volume is turned up.

match a Reason track to other recorded material that had itself been recorded out of tune. Under the Audio Card setting you choose which device to use
to fire sound out of Reason. In practice you'll probably only have one sound
card active, and you should choose it from the list.

The Sample Rate option is based on the available rates supported by your
soundcard. Low end cards will support up to 44.1kHz, higher spec ones up to
96kHz and some even up to 192kHz. As a rule of thumb, work at 44.1kHz, as
this is CD quality. 48kHz is the standard for DAT and DVD but you can encounter
issues when moving files to hardware with different capabilities. Usually this
involves a track playing slower or quicker than it should for no apparent reason.
The way around this is to resample the track to a sample rate supported by the
new hardware. Equally, there's no real point in working at a sample rate of less
than 44.1kHz unless you know why you need to.

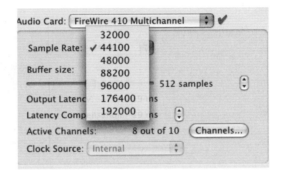

Figure 1.11
Even though some very high sample
rates may be available, you don't
normally need them.

The buffer settings control the streaming of audio between software and
hardware. Buffer size is important because it affects the latency of MIDI and
the reliability of audio playback. Latency is a small but annoying gap between
your pressing a key and hearing the sound. Too much latency can make it
impossible to play in time. Setting a lower buffer size reduces the latency but
also increases the risk of pops and clicks in the audio playback. Raising the
buffer size increases latency but makes for improved audio performance. As
all hardware setups are different there's no strict rule for what setting to use,
although a buffer size of 256 or 512 samples is often a good bet. Experiment
with settings to see what works best and gives you minimum latency but
maximum audio quality.

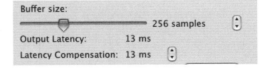

Figure 1.12
Lower buffer settings for lower latency.

Reason supports up to 64 channels of audio output and Reason 5 allows up
to 64 channels of audio input. You can see these ports on the Audio Out and
Audio In modules at the top of the rack. If your audio interface supports more
than two output channels, you can activate them in the audio preferences box
and connect instruments or mixers to them. Sound will then be routed to the
hardware outputs on your interface as you decide in the preferences.

Tip

Mac users – if you are having
trouble getting sound output,
switch the preferences to use Built
In Audio. All Macs have an internal
soundcard and at least one
speaker as standard. If you can
get sound out of the Mac speaker
but not the third-party soundcard,
the problem isn't with Reason but
with the settings of the other
device. On PC or Mac you can
always try plugging headphones
into the built-in soundcard to test
where a fault is occurring.

Tip

Here's a good rule of thumb :
when you're playing MIDI in a
lot and writing music, use a lower
buffer setting to get minimum
latency. Then when you're
arranging and mixing, increase
the buffer size to improve audio
performance. If you're not playing
notes in any more the latency
won't be an issue.

Tip

Users of Mac OS X can group
together multiple audio
interfaces using the Audio MIDI
Setup program located in
Applications > Utilities. These are
presented to software as a single
interface.

Figure 1.13
Audio driver selection on the PC.

A note about audio drivers

On a PC, audio hardware will have an ASIO driver supplied with it. Choose this driver to use with the device. Alternatively, use the DirectX or ASIO multimedia driver, but only if a specific ASIO driver isn't available.

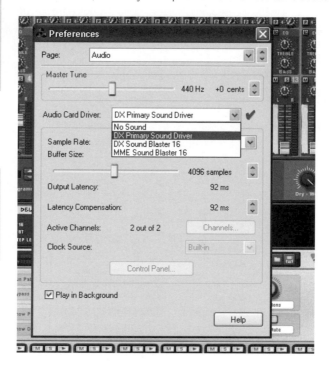

On Mac OSX, Built-in Audio should be selected to use the internal audio hardware, or the specific driver that controls your third-party device should be selected. For example if you have an M-Audio Audiophile USB, its name will appear as an option in the list for you to choose.

MIDI settings

In Reason 2.5 – for those still running old systems

From the dropdown menu you can select which device to use for MIDI input. In many cases this will be the same as the audio device, as most cards offer both audio and MIDI in and out. If you have separate audio and MIDI devices, Reason will happily use them both at the same time. There are 16 standard MIDI channels but a safe bet is to use channel 1 on all your devices when setting up communication.

Advanced MIDI lets you configure Reason to receive MIDI input from external sources for the purpose of remote control or sync. Usually you will have one MIDI interface handling all communication so that is the one to choose. If you're not syncing Reason or hooking it up to any external sequencers you don't need to worry about these settings.

In Reason 3, 4 and 5

Reason 3,4 and 5 have a MIDI tab called Control Surfaces and Keyboards. This is because they use a system of handling MIDI communication called Remote. Instead of reading from a single device, Reason can receive data from multiple MIDI controllers at the same time. The point of this is to make it much easier to play your Reason system. Instead of being predominantly a studio tool it can now be used much more easily as a live performance tool as well. Many people have a USB MIDI controller keyboard, or a standard keyboard with realtime controllers like knobs and sliders. Reason has built-in support for a wide range of controllers from leading manufacturers, and allows you to customise setups for keyboards that aren't supported out of the box. Support for new models will be added as they come onto the market. As templates are stored in a folder independent of the program itself, this will not require any program updates but rather a simple drag-and-drop. Here are some things to note about the Remote system.

Tip

A good way to check that MIDI is being received is to hit some notes on the keyboard and look at the channel 1 section of Reason's MIDI panel. You should see a red light blink when you play. If not, check your keyboard is sending on channel 1 and Reason is receiving from the correct device on channel 1 .

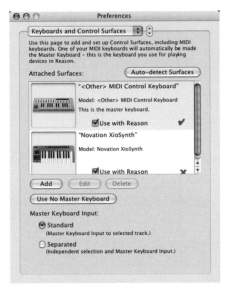

Figure 1.14
Reason 4 and 5 can recognise and use multiple MIDI input devices at once. You can now record multiple MIDI channels at once but only with Reason 5.

When you install and boot Reason for the first time it will scan your system for any installed drivers relating to MIDI controller devices. If you are adding devices with drivers later, there is an auto-detect button on the Preferences > Control Surfaces dialogue box.

If Reason does pick up such a device, it will automatically map its realtime knobs and sliders to the most useful controls on whichever module in the rack you select. Typically, sliders will correspond to mixer channels or filter controls on an instrument. Knobs on a keyboard will probably be mapped to filter or pan controls. You can remap these, but for everyday purposes the default settings are useful. When you get into locking surfaces later on, you may also have a choice of using two different built-in mapping configurations, depending on your controller and the device you're trying to control.

In the list of attached surfaces you can specify by ticking or unticking the box whether each should be used with Reason. You may have a controller

Auto-detect Surfaces

Figure 1.15
Auto-Detect Surfaces.

Tip

If you select a controller device from the list of available models, look out for any information that is displayed next to its picture in the Control Surface setup window. Some devices have idiosyncracies that need to be remembered when setting up, such as a particular setting that has to be made or a channel that has to be active.

Tip

In Reason 5, with multiple MIDI devices connected you can now record notes on different sequencer tracks as well as just automation data.

accessing another program and not want it to interfere with Reason. In this situation, uncheck the box. The Add, Edit and Delete buttons let you manage your list of controllers.

If your MIDI keyboard is not picked up, or is connected via a MIDI interface rather than USB or FireWire, you can make Reason pick it up by clicking the Add button. Select the manufacturer or choose Other if it isn't displayed. Then from the Model menu choose what kind of keyboard it is. If your MIDI interface is not automatically picked up, press the Find button and press a key on the keyboard. Using MIDI Learn, Reason will pick it up and remember it.

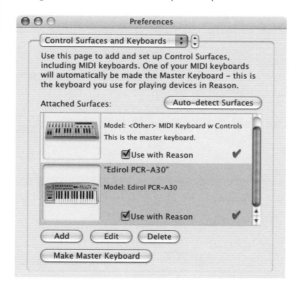

Figure 1.16
Use the Add menu to add further controllers to use with Reason.

Figure 1.16a Reason 5 allows you to use computer keys as MIDI input, for when there's no physical keyboard available.

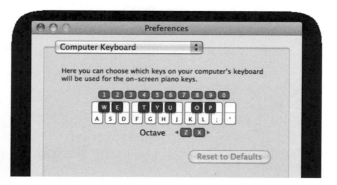

Figure 1.17
Locking devices to modules in the rack allows more hands-on control by several people.

The more realtime controllers you have on your keyboard, the better your control over Reason will be. A small keyboard will offer basic controls, but a bigger one like the M-Audio Keystation Pro 88 or a dedicated control surface like a Mackie Control will give you much more comprehensive options if you happen to own one. Reason even supports motorized faders and device naming on dedicated control surfaces.

The way to manage the multiple devices is to lock them to devices in the rack. The controller specified as the Master Keyboard in the preferences will always follow the MIDI input (i.e. play whichever module you select in the rack). However, any number of subsequent controllers can be added. By selecting Options > Surface Locking you can select any available controller and lock it to any available module. This means it will always just control that module, at least until you unlock them from each other. In the preferences you can choose Standard or Separated mode for the Master Keyboard, governing whether it always follows track selection or works independently of track selection.

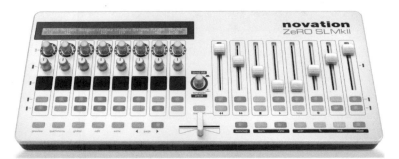

Figure 1.18
A USB MIDI controller locked to the mixer is a great way of 'playing' your system.

In use

By having more than one control surface connected at once you can greatly extend the usefulness of Reason. Here are a couple of examples.

The most obvious application for the Remote system is to have several people controlling the same Reason system off the same computer at the same time. With several USB keyboards connected, or several MIDI keyboards via an interface, or a mixture of the two systems, you can share the same project. By locking each device to a module you can all have independent control over tweaking your own instruments in realtime. This is particularly interesting if you are using Combinator patches with sequencers inside them. As Reason outputs usually to a single stereo out, the sum total of your performance can be put through a single stereo amp channel.

Another interesting application would be to have a controller locked to the mixer, and a keyboard then playing whatever you point it at. In this way you can have control over the mix of a project including solo and mute, pan, levels and effects settings as it is playing and as you are playing along with it.In Reason 5 you are now able to record not just automation for additional connected MIDI controllers but also record MIDI notes for them as well.

You can mix and match these ideas to have, say, control over the mixer and several instruments yourself, but with further people controlling other instruments from the same project.

If you discover that the auto-mapping isn't quite to your taste, or you have a more generic MIDI controller keyboard, you can re-map controls easily. By selecting Options > Remote Override Edit Mode you can choose a module in the rack to map. The modules are greyed out, and coloured symbols denote the parameters that can be mapped. If you double-click on a parameter it displays a lightning bolt. When you move a controller on your keyboard, or press a note, Reason maps that note or switch to the parameter you have selected.

If you control + click or right-click on a parameter in this mode, a sepa-

Figure 1.19
Re-mapping realtime controllers to
controls on Reason's modules.

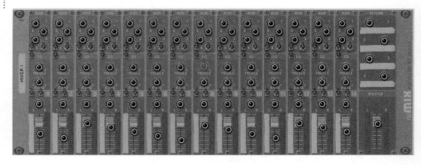

rate window appears to let you choose specifically which controller device
should be used, and which type of control message should be read. By clicking the Learn button here you can see precisely what type of control you are
pressing or turning on your keyboard. Once a control has been mapped, this
window will also let you edit that mapping.

Even keys on the keyboard can be used as triggers, although they work
as on/off switches rather than variables. Mapping a key to a knob or slider
and then pressing it will change values between zero and 100 per cent. So
you could for example have part of a keyboard or even a dedicated keyboard
with controls mapped simply to muting and enabling channels, switching
effects on and off or bypassing devices entirely.

Figure 1.20
Keyboard Control Mode.

There is an additional menu of extra, system-specific overrides that you
can map independently by selecting Options > Additional Remote Overrides.
These include undo / redo, auto-quantize, patch selection and so on. With a
bit of planning and some sticky labels on your keys to remind you what they
trigger, you can control almost every aspect of a Reason song in a live setting without ever touching the mouse.

Sound locations

Reason 2.5 – for those running old systems

When you open a patch or file browser in Reason there are some special
shortcut buttons available. The four folder buttons correspond to sound locations set in the preferences. It's good practice to keep your ReFills and sam-

ples properly organized in a few folders, or even just in one. In the Sound Locations preference page, you can set up to four locations that Reason will remember and the buttons in the file browser will jump you straight to those folders. This can save you a huge amount of time in wandering around your hard drive looking for files.

A good way to organize sounds might be to have one folder for ReFills, one for samples and one for your own patches. Hit the cross next to the location buttons to delete the links and specify a new one.

Reason 3, 4 and 5

In Reason 3 and 4 the Sound Locations section is removed. This function is now incorporated into the new browser. See the next chapter for detailed information on this.

Working methods

Inside the Reason folder are a number of PDF files, including the Operation Manual and some notes about the effect devices. Although it may seem a bit tedious to go through it, it's worth at least one read through to familiarise yourself with some of the terminology and concepts used in the program. The manual is very well written and fairly exhaustive. If you're using Acrobat or Preview (Mac OSX only) to read the PDF, as you probably will be, don't forget the search functions. Typing a word or a sentence into the search box will show all instances of the words in the document. This is sometimes better than relying on chapter headings to find information.

Figure 2.1
Always read the manual at least once!

15

The Concept

Figure 2.2

The rack, sequencer, ReGroove mixer and transport.

It's fairly clear that Reason is based on the idea of a rack of instruments and effects. This makes it easier to get the hang of, and as an added bonus it looks pretty cool as well. It's designed to look familiar while retaining the advantages of using software – for example the ability to save and load, to

duplicate, copy and paste and to have as many modules as your hardware can run. Think of it as halfway between software and hardware. Faders, buttons and switches all move like they do in real life. On the other hand, menus and file browsers offer the kind of speedy workflow that you can't get with real instruments.

The Windows

Real hardware, of course, has things on the back of it like ports and master controls. Pressing the Tab key rotates the rack 180 degrees so that you can use them. Reason's window can be extended upwards and downwards, but not left or right. Pressing the small button at the extreme top right of the window will detach the sequencer from the rack. This can also be done by selecting Windows > Detach Sequencer Window. This is particularly useful for navigating projects as it means you can have more of the timeline on the screen. There's no facility for the rack to extend outwards, as the modules are all a set width. The sequencer, however, can be zoomed and scrolled. This is handy if you're in Edit mode. If you're very lucky and have two monitors, use one screen for the rack and one for the sequencer.

The line that divides the rack and the sequencer can be dragged up or down to alter the proportion of space taken up by each side. To maximise the sequencer, click the small button at the top right of its section. To maximise the rack, click the similar button at its top right corner. Click either again to return to a split screen. Being able to maximise the sequencer in Edit mode is great when you have to view multiple controller lanes and data at the same time.

Things to remember

Reason is a MIDI sequencer. You can't record audio straight into it as conventional audio tracks though you can now sample in as much real audio as you like. It's self-contained and doesn't support external plugins of any kind. A Reason song file doesn't contain any audio tracks – consisting of MIDI, it's mostly a series of instructions. Any audio samples that you record are stored inside the song file for convenience. So if you move projects between machines, your instrument sounds won't go with you unless you make a point of copying the ReFills and samples as well.The exception is samples you record yourself, which will be transferred.

There are often a number of ways of achieving the same goal in Reason. Usually these are by dropdown menu or by contextual menu, and sometimes by keyboard shortcut or via the Tool Window. Most things in Reason are contextual, which means that you get different options depending on what you've clicked on. For example, control + clicking somewhere in the rack brings up one menu, but control + clicking on the sequencer brings up another. The part of the window that you select is outlined in light blue, which is how to tell which part you're working on. If you perform a command such as delete, and the wrong thing disappears, it's probably because you had something selected other than the item you wanted to delete. It's good practice to click on a module or a sequencer track once to make sure it's selected before you start modifying it.

The Tool Window in Reason 5 is a great way to quickly access all kinds of functions. Its first tab is Devices, and you can drag and drop any module from

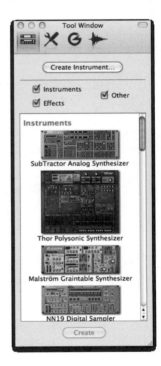

Info

Reason's rack is, in theory, endless. It will literally house as many instruments and effects as your computer can cope with. As your mixer runs out of channels, create a second mixer and chain it to the first.

Tip

Press the Tab key to spin the rack around, and again to spin it back.

Tip

Choose Options > Show Cables to show and hide the patch cables linking the modules.

Info

ReFills are special Reason Soundbanks containing all the patches and audio files you need to make music. They aren't folders and they aren't programs, and can't be opened except from within Reason, via an instrument or effect module.

Info

There are lots of free and commercial ReFills available for download or mail order. A lot of major sample CD companies now release their sounds in ReFill as well as other formats.

here straight into the rack. Check the boxes to show instruments or effects. The Create Instrument button takes you straight to the Browser. The Tools tab duplicates many of the functions found in the Edit and contextual right click menus and mostly relates to any notes or groups selected in the sequencer. Crucial commands like quantize and editing pitch and velocity can be quickly used from here. It's a great way to view settings all in one place and also make multiple changes in one go, for example transposing several groups of notes. The Groove tab relates to the ReGroove mixer and duplicates the settings found on its panel. Use the channel selector menu to choose a slot, then make the relevant settings. if you click the Get From Clip button with a group of notes selected, Reason will extract the timing and groove from it and make it available to be used or saved. The Tool Window is quickly shown or hidden with the F8 key. The final tab, found only in Reason 5, allows you to manage, edit and view the audio samples involved in a project, including both samples from ReFills and samples that you have recorded yourself.

Figure 2.3
Detach the two elements, rack and sequencer. Spread them over two screens if you can!

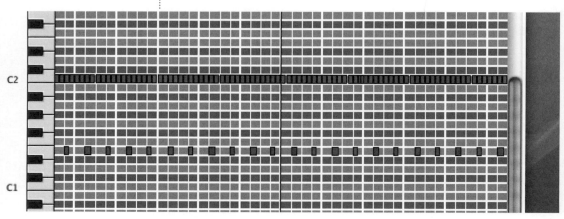

Figure 2.4
Reason works with MIDI, triggering audio samples and generating synthesized sounds.

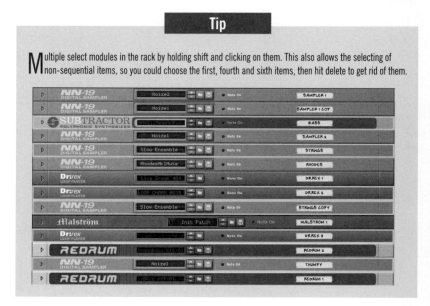

Tip

Multiple select modules in the rack by holding shift and clicking on them. This also allows the selecting of non-sequential items, so you could choose the first, fourth and sixth items, then hit delete to get rid of them.

Figure 2.5
Selecting non-sequential modules.

The Transport panel

The Transport panel is always present, even if you split up the two sections. It contains all the tools you need to control playback and recording. It can actually be minimized so as to be almost invisible by clicking the small arrow on its far right hand side, but it takes up so little space anyway that you won't end up hiding it very often, if ever. The main Transport panel controls are the same as the controls on a tape machine. Basic operations like play, stop and record are mapped to simple key presses.

Tempo and time signature

The left tempo field is where you set the tempo from 1 to 999 beats per minute. Typically, ambient music is around 75-95 BPM, hip hop around 80-100BPM and dance music 100BPM and above. The field on the right lets you set very precise divisions of 1/1000BPM, if you need for some reason to have an odd speed. Using the plus and minus keys on the numeric keypad will increase or decrease the tempo in increments of 1BPM (Figure 2.6).

Click the time signature up / down arrows to control the master time signature. 4/4 is by far the most commonly used timebase, but you are by no means limited to it. Tracks with unusual time signatures often sound more interesting. The grid and the click will change to follow the new values if you alter them.

Tempo and time signature automation

Reason 4 and 5 support tempo and time signature automation - a great system with all sorts of applications. In the sequencer, if you select the new Transport lane and activate its record Enable Parameter Automation button, then click on the Automation dropdown menu you will see tempo and time signature available as options (Figure 2.6a). Activate either and you can draw in tempo changes using the pencil tool. Using the pointer and the resulting

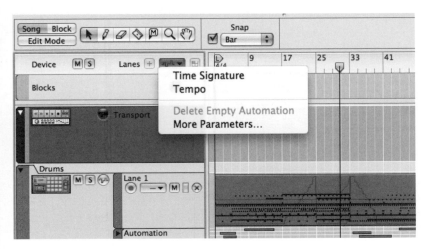

Figure 2.6
Setting the Tempo.

Figure 2.6a

vector automation points you can create groups containing tempo change data to speed up or slow down the track to any extent and as as often as you like (Figure 2.6b). Once the playhead moves outside the group – the shaded area – it will return to the root tempo as indicated by the blue line. To

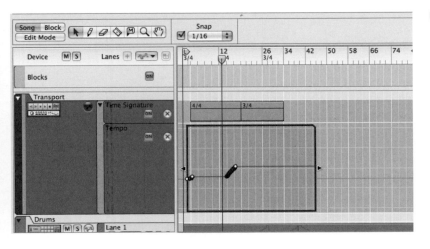

Figure 2.6b.

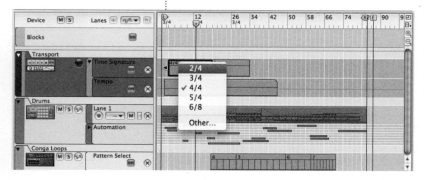

Figure 2.6c

automate time signature, draw groups into the sequencer track and then choose a defined signature by clicking on the value field. These can't change gradually like tempo so have to move from one to another (Figure 2.6c). If the playhead moves outside a clip containing time signature information, it will default back to 4/4 so unless this is your goal, clips must run edge to edge. Modifying tempo is an excellent way to create dynamic tracks or match Reason projects to film or TV. Changing tempo or time signature on the fly is a good way to surprise listeners, especially when playing live.

Locators

The left and right locators are incredibly useful. A lot of the time it's necessary to loop sections while you build up layers of music. The locators tell Reason where to start and end loops, as well as how much to export when you've finished. There are several ways to set locator positions (Figure 2.7).

- Pick up and drag the locators on the timeline
- Double click the number fields in the transport panel and enter a numerical value for where you want it to go. The fields are divided by bar and beat. So entering 12.2.1 would put the locator at the second beat of bar 12.
- Click and hold the mouse on a number field and drag the pointer up or down, or left and right. Doing this on the left field scrolls quickest, on the middle field it's slower and on the right field slowest but most precise.
- Alt + click on the bar display in the timeline to set the left locator. Option + click to set the right locator. Shift + click in the same area to set the end marker for the whole project. The end marker can be dragged further to the right to extend the overall length of a project.
- Pressing the L and R buttons on the Transport bar now jump you straight to the relevant locators on the timeline. New readouts show you bars, beats and ticks and also the length of a project in hours, minutes, seconds and miliseconds. Double click and enter a value in any of these fields to jump to it in the project.

Other Transport tricks

The Click track, which will be crucial to recording in time, is switched on and off, and its level set, from the Transport Panel (Figure 2.8).

If sounds are starting to distort, check the Audio Out Clipping indicator on the Transport Panel. If it has lit up, the hardware interface is being fed levels that are too high. Try reducing the level of individual mixer channels or the master fader level. Level meters should be in the yellow and orange but not the red (Figure 2.9).

The CPU level indicator is not an absolute measure of CPU use. For example if it read 100%, it would not mean that Reason was using the computer's whole capacity. It displays how much power Reason's audio engine is using. Audio processing gets priority over graphics and MIDI, which have to share what's left over. If this meter is pushing into the red, it's time to simplify your song or buy a faster computer.

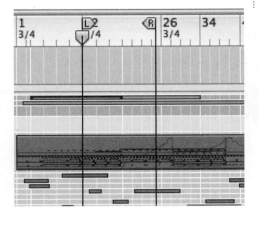

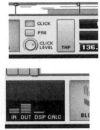

Figure 2.7 (left)
The left and right locators are crucial to working in Reason.

Figure 2.8 (top)
The all-important click control.

Figure 2.9 (bottom)
The Audio Clipping Indicator.

Reason 4 and 5 have a couple of new elements to the Transport Panel. The New Dub button adds a new note lane to the selected track but doesn't mute the previous lane - great for keeping notes separate whilst recording but also building loops on top of what you've just played. The New Alt button creates a new lane but does mute the previous take - better for trying multiple takes or versions of a loop then identifying the best one later. There's also a new pre-count button next to the click button, which when activated will give you a one bar click before starting recording when you press the record button. In Reason 5 there's a Quantize During Record option, which quantizes parts as you record them. Finally, the 'Automation as Perf Control' button in Reason 4, when active, causes any automation like pitch bend or mod wheel to be recorded not into a new automation lane but straight into the note clip. This makes it easier to move the clip plus its associated automation data in one go.

The Hardware Interface

This is where you manage how Reason communicates with the rest of your system. Divided into two sections, the Hardware Interface (Figure 2.10) can't be deleted, and so is always present in the rack. Reason always has to be able to transmit sound and realistically will always have to receive MIDI, so you'll always need the hardware interface. It is split into two sections.

MIDI In Device

- Reason can accept up to 64 channels of MIDI input. This is split into 4 busses, each with 16 MIDI channels.
- The most common way of routing MIDI is via the Sequencer. When you select a track, the device connected to that track will automatically receive MIDI input. A green level meter on the sequencer track will light to show MIDI received.
- Using this method, you only need set the master MIDI channel once in the preferences, and MIDI in will go to whichever instrument you select.
- If you have a more advanced MIDI interface, you can use the preferences to set up to four MIDI input busses, each with 16 channels. This is the mode to

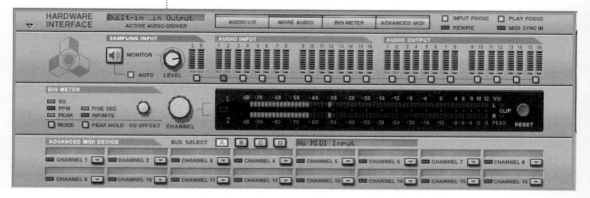

Figure 2.10
The hardware interface.

use if you want to control Reason's instruments from an external sequencer, or send information on several MIDI channels at once.

- In this mode, you have to use the dropdown menu by each MIDI in channel to specify which instrument to route signal to. A list of all available instrument modules will appear in the dropdown list.
- A red LED blinking by each MIDI channel indicates MIDI received on that channel. If it isn't coming through correctly, check that your keyboard or sequencer is transmitting on the correct channel and that Reason's preferences are set correctly to receive.
- You can use the bus select buttons at the top of the interface to choose which of the four busses is on view.
- With the new Remote system, multiple MIDI in devices can be used at the same time.

Audio In and Out Devices

- Reason allows for up to 64 channels of audio output and 64 channels of audio input, if your hardware has that many. In reality you probably won't use more than 8 or 10 channels unless you're using ReWire.
- You activate the outputs in the Preferences > Audio window. Use the Active Channels button.

> **Tip**
>
> In Reason 4 and 5 the Hardware interface is colour coded. A green light denotes a channel in use, yellow means an output is available to a sound card or ReWire channel, and red means a cable may be connected but there is currently no destination. No light means a channel is off.

Figure 2.11
The MIDI interface lets you manage multiple MIDI inputs.

- One use for multiple outputs is if you are routing sound out of Reason to an external mixing desk or through outboard effects. By setting up tracks to fire straight out of your soundcard's outputs, say, drum tracks to a compressor and pads to a reverb unit, you could process them externally.
- If you do this, it's best to do the whole track through an external mixer, as getting the processed sound back into Reason in realtime would be tricky.
- You can still use Reason's effects and mixer before sending sound through hardware outputs, creating a signal chain. This is due to its modular nature, and the fact that you can pick up and re-patch cables as you like. Just follow the chain through to make sure the sound is being sent to and from the right place.

- The most likely use for the 64 outputs is with ReWire, where audio is streamed from Reason into the mixer of another sequencer such as Cubase, Logic or SONAR.

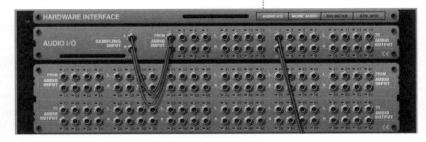

- The most likely use for more than a couple of audio input channels being connected is if you wanted to have multiple hardware devices like a mic, a keyboard and a guitar all able to be recorded at the drop of a hat. Assign inputs using the Audio > Preferences menu.

Figure 2.12
From the Audio Out panel you can route any audio signal to your soundcard, or to ReWire. The audio inputs are used for sampling.

The Browser

Reason sports a great browser (Figure 2.13), which had remained much the same up to big changes introduced in version 3. Now it's almost like a program within a program. Made up of different regions, it has a number of new search and preview functions.

Figure 2.13
The new Browser, much extended.

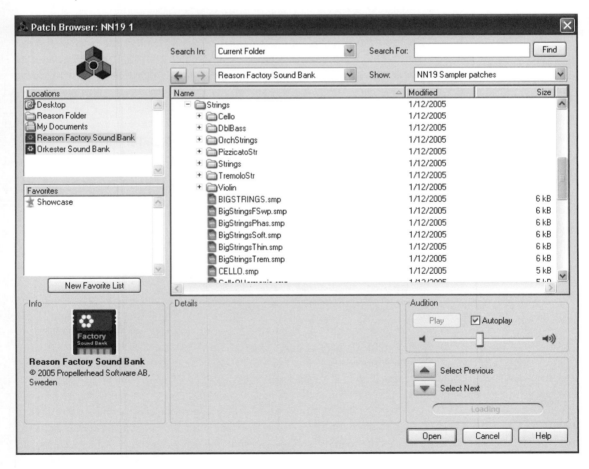

Figure 2.14
Set up and name favourites lists
containing patches and samples.

The Sound Locations tab from versions prior to 3 has been moved to the Browser. By navigating to a folder on your hard drive and drag + dropping it into the Locations window you can build up a list of folder shortcuts with no limit on the number of folders. To remove items from this list, control+click or right-click and select Remove.

To save time when locating your favourite patches, use the Favourites window (Figure 2.14). Create a new list, right-click or control+click to rename it and then drag any number of your favourite patches to the list for instant location. This is useful when playing live or for inspiration when composing on-the-fly.

The search section at the top is very powerful and lets you be very specific about the files you find. The first level of filtering is by location type. These go from the narrow (search current folder) to medium (search within User Locations) to the broad (search all local disks). The two arrows will take you back or forward through all the locations you have previously searched during that session.

To jump to a hierarchical view of the computer's disks, choose Desktop from the Locations list. Then, the dropdown menu will allow access to all levels of the drives. To save time, drop local hard drives into the Locations window so that they are accessible with a single click.

Reason's browser can navigate to any volume, be it an internal or FireWire hard drive, CD / DVD, USB flash drive, networked volume or even iPod. It can load sounds from any of these. However, if any of these are disconnected later, Reason won't be able to find the sounds. Remember a Reason project

Figure 2.15
Advanced searching.

file only contains links to sounds, not the sounds themselves, unless you have recorded samples in Reason 5. Working from CD or networked volume will also slow you down considerably. A much better idea is to keep everything on internal hard drives.

One of the greatest features in Reason is that the Browser actually loads patches as you select them, meaning you can play and hear them from within the Browser itself! Before, you had to actually load the whole patch into the rack to hear what it sounded like, which could result in a lot of time spent going through patches, deciding they weren't appropriate and then browsing and loading again until you found one. That's now a thing of the past. As patches are selected they are loaded automatically. Samples and REX files are previewed as you select them. You can switch Autoplay on or off and manually stop or start samples and set volume using the Audition window. The volume slider controls the levels of audio files that audition, not MIDI-triggered instruments.

The same applies to effects. You can't 'play' an effect but you can play through it. So if you have a guitar sound loaded into an NN-XT, for example, then attach an effect unit to it, you can use the browser to audition different effect patches for that module. As you move between them, keep playing the keyboard and you'll hear the guitar sound effected in different ways. This is the case with every effect module.

The Search For text box lets you perform a text search for patches and files. This is very useful because it will find all files containing the word(s) you enter, regardless of file type. For example, if you search for 'Bass' you will be presented with every file containing the word Bass. You can limit this by using the Show menu to specify whether to view all instruments, all effects or Combinator patches. If you're browsing for an effect patch you won't want to see all the instrument patches, just the effects. Furthermore, the results can be sorted by clicking the column names. For example, to sort them by style click the Parent column. For an alphabetical list, click the Name column and so on. The Browser also displays helpful information in the Details section about each patch you select, although this tends to be more relevant for Combinator patches.

When you browse from a certain type of device, the Show menu will alter to reflect that. If you browse from a Subtractor for instance, it will default to showing only Subtractor patches because this is probably what you're after. However you can always switch this menu to show all instruments, displaying all patches for all modules.

You don't have to enter any text to search. For example, if you browse from an RV-7000 effect module and then select

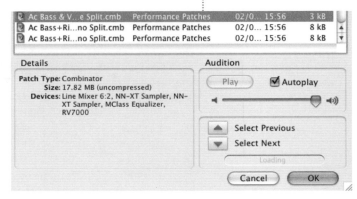

Figure 2.16
You can preview sounds in the Browser in Reason.

Figure 2.17
Sorting search results by column.

Name	Parent	Modified	Size
Pusher Upright Bass.cmb	Acoustic Bass	02/0... 15:56	4 kB
Upright Bass.sxt	Acoustic Bass	02/0... 15:56	29 kB
Upright II.sxt	Acoustic Bass	02/0... 15:56	18 kB
Upright Old...htclub.cmb	Acoustic Bass	02/0... 15:56	3 kB
Upright Old...htclub.cmb	Acoustic Bass	02/0... 15:56	3 kB
Upright+Harm.sxt	Acoustic Bass	02/0... 15:56	38 kB
UprightHarmonics.sxt	Acoustic Bass	02/0... 15:56	9 kB
Ac TightNBassy.sxt	Acoustic Guitar	02/0... 15:56	21 kB
2StepBass.xwv	Bass	02/0... 15:56	1 kB
4am Bass.zyp	Bass	02/0... 15:56	1 kB
80s Syn bass.xwv	Bass	02/0... 15:56	1 kB
AcBss MW Mute.zyp	Bass	02/0... 15:56	1 kB

Search in User Locations and Show RV7000 patches but don't enter anything into the text field, you will get a list of every patch within your Location folders that can be loaded by this module. The same applies to any other module.

Searching Local Disks, or having an entire drive (like Macintosh HD or the C: drive) in the Locations list can considerably slow down a search for files, as Reason has to sort through thousands of files. It's a much better idea to keep patches and sounds in individual folders and put these in the Favourites list, so Reason isn't having to scour pointless system and library folders. In this case you must also of course use the Search In User Locations or Current Folder options.

You can create devices directly from the Browser, regardless of the type of module you browsed from. For example, let's say you browse in from a Subtractor. You search for 'Lead' and find a great Lead synth patch, but it's for a Malström. Where previously you would have had to go back a load a Malström, then re-browse, now you can just load one by pressing OK in the browser. In fact, as you audition different patches you can see that Reason loads the relevant module in the rack, replacing the module you browsed from.

When you run a search for a particular word and view the results in a list, you can use the folder dropdown menu (next to the two arrows) to jump to the parent folder of that patch. This is because such a search can turn up varied results. Jumping to the parent folder of a patch will show you what category it is in as well as giving you quick access to other patches in that category (Figure 2.18).

Figure 2.18

Jump to the parent folder of a patch to see patches of similar type.

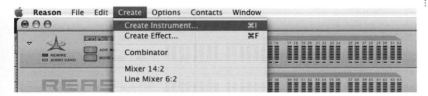

Figure 2.19
Create devices of a certain type from the Create menu

There are items in the Create menu called Create Instrument and Create Effect. Essentially, if you start from anywhere in the rack (even an empty rack), you can browse for any kind of patch, audition it and Reason will load it in the background. This is great for creativity and spontenaiety as it means you don't have to create a device and then decide on a sound, you can browse a whole palette of sounds and be inspired (Figure 2.19). You can also drag devices straight from the new Tool window to put them quickly into the rack, though you then have to select a patch within the device.

If you browse from the sample section (not patch section) of an NN-19 and find a REX file, you can expand that REX file within the browser to see

Figure 2.20
Browse from the sample load button of a sampler and you can view and load the individual slices of REX files.

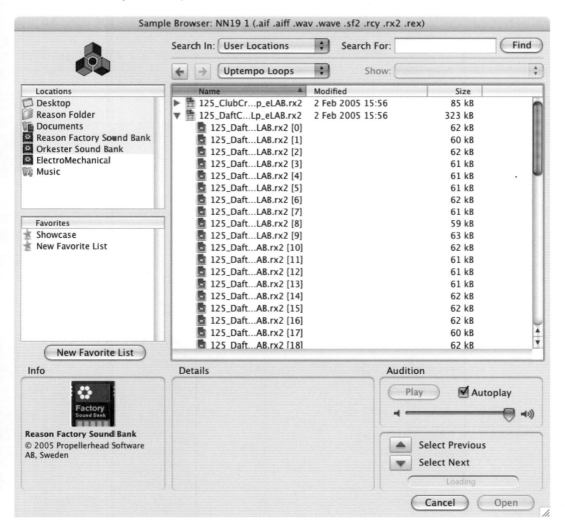

its constituent parts, and then load a single slice into the NN-19. The same applies if you browse from the sample button (not patch button) on any channel in a ReDrum.

Creating devices

Reason projects are constructed by creating devices in the rack, then playing MIDI into the sequencer, which has tracks connected to those devices. Before you can hear any sounds you have to create some modules. A few points to remember about devices:

- Reason has a set number of devices and doesn't support third-party plugins of any kind. However, because modules can be freely patched together, it is still a very flexible program.
- The Audio and MIDI interfaces at the top of the rack are always present. The Audio Input device can be used to manage how sound is routed in for the purposes of sampling.
- You can create as many devices as your computer can handle. Some are more power-hungry than others, so 50 ReDrums is not the same power drain as 50 Malströms. Different patches for the same instrument also use different amounts of power.
- Like a real studio setup, everything in Reason runs through a mixer. You're not limited to one mixer – several can be chained together.
- Everything can be unplugged and re-patched, and there's no limit on how many stages a source can go through before it reaches the desk. For example, a sampler could run through one, ten or fifty effect modules before it got to the desk.

The simplest way to create a device is to go to the Create menu at the top and select which kind of device to insert. Or, drag a device on from the Tool window. You should always start with a mixer. Otherwise, the first instrument you create will be wired straight to the hardware interface, and subsequent instruments you create won't output any sound until connected to more audio outputs on the hardware interface. Whilst this works and is possible, it's a labour-intensive way to use Reason. It's far better to use a mixer.

Reason automatically routes the outputs of instruments into the mixer. This means that you can create a device and know that it will be plugged into the next available mixer channel for you. If you have disconnected a device (Edit > Disconnect Device) or re-patched it and want it routed straight back into the mixer, select it and choose Edit > Auto-Route Device, and Reason will re-patch it into the next available mixer channel.

There's no set order in which you have to create devices, although it makes sense to have the mixer at the top (Figure 3.2).

Figure 3.1
The Create menu.

Create Instrument...	⌘I
Create Effect...	⌘F
Combinator	
Mixer 14:2	
Line Mixer 6:2	
SubTractor Analog Synthesizer	
Thor Polysonic Synthesizer	
Malström Graintable Synthesizer	
NN19 Digital Sampler	
NN-XT Advanced Sampler	
Dr. Octo Rex Loop Player	
Redrum Drum Computer	
Kong Drum Designer	
MClass Mastering Suite Combi	
MClass Equalizer	
MClass Stereo Imager	
MClass Compressor	
MClass Maximizer	
RV7000 Advanced Reverb	
Scream 4 Distortion	
BV512 Digital Vocoder	
RV-7 Digital Reverb	
DDL-1 Digital Delay Line	
D-11 Foldback Distortion	
ECF-42 Envelope Controlled Filter	
CF-101 Chorus/Flanger	
PH-90 Phaser	
UN-16 Unison	
COMP-01 Compressor/Limiter	
PEQ-2 Two Band Parametric EQ	
Spider Audio Merger & Splitter	
Spider CV Merger & Splitter	
Matrix Pattern Sequencer	
RPG-8 Monophonic Arpeggiator	
ReBirth Input Machine	

Figure 3.2
Auto-routing devices if they have been disconnected.

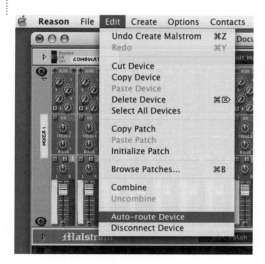

Tips for working with devices

- Deleting devices is as simple as selecting them and hitting backspace. Also you can select the device and select Edit > Delete Device.
- Press command + delete (Mac) or control + delete (PC) to get rid of a device without the confirmation box popping up.
- Hold down shift + click to select multiple and non-sequential devices in the rack.
- Each module has a small arrow at the top left corner. Click on it to expand or minimize the device. Alt + clicking it will expand or minimize every device in the rack at once. This saves a lot of time when working with many devices in a rack. It also works when the rack is spun around.
- Instrument devices can be dragged up and down and re-ordered in the rack, but only when they are picked up by their end panels, between the screws. This works whether they are minimized or maximized. They can also be re-ordered in the sequencer. Neither of these operations alters the order in which they are connected to the mixer.
- Control + click (Mac) or right click (PC) on an empty section of the rack brings up the same menu as you get from the Create option at the top (Figure 3.3).
- If you delete a device connected between two devices, Reason automatically compensates by reconnecting the two remaining devices. So for example if you have a sampler running into a reverb unit and then on into the mixer, then you delete the reverb unit, the sampler will be patched directly into the mixer.
- If you duplicate a device in the rack by dragging it or using copy and paste, it is not automatically routed. If you want it to be, hold down the Shift key as you drag / copy.
- If you re-order a device by dragging it up or down the rack, it stays plugged into the same mixer channel. If you want it to move to a different mixer channel based on its new position in the rack, hold down Shift while you drag it.

Figure 3.3
The contextual menu.

- To force Reason not to auto-route a device when you create it, hold down the Shift key.
- Using the up and down arrows on the keyboard will quickly scroll up or down the rack, selecting modules as you go.

Types of devices

Reason has two main types of modules – instruments and effects. Within these there are some subdivisions. Some of the instruments are synthesizers, which generate sounds, and some are sample-based, meaning that they use existing audio samples to play back sounds. Of the effect devices, most apply an effect to an audio signal, but a couple are routing modules which send CV signal rather than audio. Sample-based modules tend to be less power hungry. Synth modules use more CPU, especially if a patch uses lots of oscillators and filters.

Tip

The Tool Window, shown by pressing F8, lets you drop devices directly into the rack without using any menus.

Cables

Patch cables show you how things are connected to each other. They are visible when you spin the rack around to view the back.

Figure 3.4
Reason's lifeblood – the patch cables.

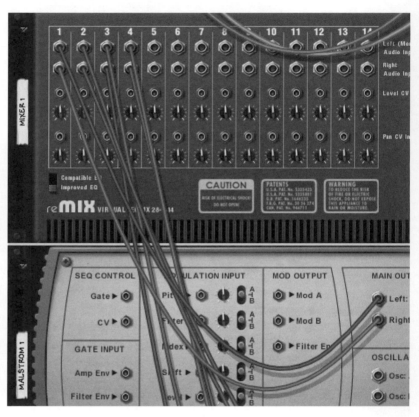

Tip

Select Options > Show Cables or press Command + L (Mac) or Control + L (PC) to toggle their visibility on and off. Useful if many cables are obscuring your view.

Tip

It can be frustrating trying to track a patch cable from source to destination. Leave the mouse pointer over a connection for a few seconds and a tooltip will appear, telling you where the cable goes.

Cables can be picked up and plugged in at either end. Audio cables and ports are larger, CV cables and ports are smaller. You can't plug an audio lead into a CV port or vice versa, as the two carry different types of signal. Cables are also colour coded for convenience.

- Audio cables are different shades of red
- CV connections are shown in shades of yellow
- Connections to and from effects modules are shown in green.

As well as clicking on a port to plug a cable into it, you can click or right-click on a port. A list of all the devices in the rack will appear. From this menu you can choose any available port on any device which will accept the connection you're trying to make. The device you're connecting from will be greyed out, as will any devices which won't accept connections from your selected module. This menu also has a Disconnect option. Disconnecting can also be done by picking up a cable and dragging it away from a jack plug.

The instrument modules have different types of outputs. The Subtractor, for example, is a monophonic instrument and so only has one output. The Dr:Rex, Malström and NN-19 have stereo audio outputs, and the ReDrum

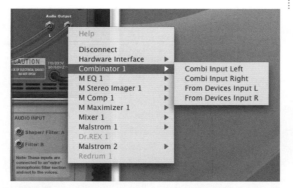

Figure 3.5
The contextual menu for a port displays all connections in the project to which that signal could be routed.

Tip

As you drag a cable over ports, suitable ones will light up in red. If a port doesn't light up, you can't connect that particular cable to it.

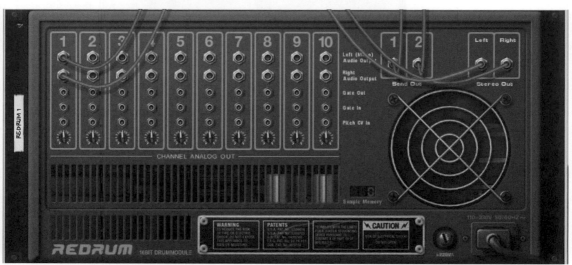

Figure 3.6
Certain modules like the ReDrum and NN-XT have separate audio outputs for their many channels.

and NN-XT sampler have multiple separate audio outputs, although used in a simple way they only need a stereo pair.

ReWire

Reason doesn't record audio tracks, but this is something that you will probably want to do when you're making music. Reason 5 is able to sample into any module where you see a sampler button. Being able to put vocals or live instruments over your Reason tracks is fairly crucial to a lot of people. You can of course mix a track down from Reason and import it into another program to overlay more sounds, but then you lose all editability on the Reason track. You can sample live into Reason 5, though it's not the ideal way to add vocal tracks or anything of any great length, since samples work best when they are fairly short.

Happily, Reason incorporates a technology called ReWire which allows it to be synchronized with other sequencers. It has a number of features:

- ReWire allows the streaming of separate audio channels between audio applications. For example, between Reason and Cubase. Up to 256 are supported.

Figure 3.7
Reason ReWired to Cubase.

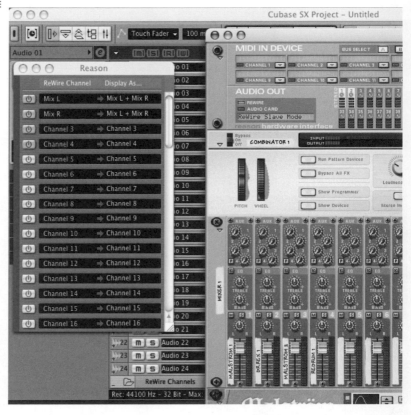

- Both programs synchronize together perfectly, and the transport controls from one will control the other. So pressing play in Cubase will also play Reason. Moving the playhead in Reason will move it to the same position in Cubase and so on.
- Both programs can share the same sound card, which can otherwise sometimes be problematic when using two applications with ASIO drivers.
- ReWire is mostly automatic and doesn't require any setting up.

Info

The ReWire system runs not from the Reason application itself but from a number of support files installed on your system. Don't move or trash any files from the Reason folder as it may disable the program.

Info

Reason is the ReWire Slave. The other sequencer, like Logic, Cubase or SONAR, is the ReWire Master. Reason always slaves to a Master when in ReWire mode.

All ReWire connections from Reason are done through the hardware interface at the top of the rack. It's a lot like what happens if you route audio straight out to the outputs of a soundcard, only in this case rather than a soundcard, the signal is sent to the mixer of your Master program, such as Cubase. Master programs generally automatically detect the presence of Reason and add it to their options menus without you having to do anything.

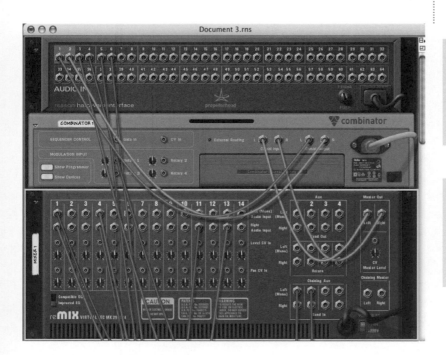

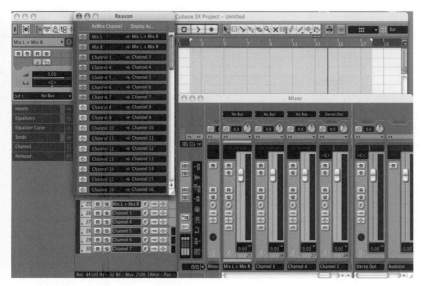

Figure 3.9 (top)
Some instruments being sent directly out to ReWire from Reason...

Figure 3.10 (left)
...and received in Cubase.

Any ReWire Master program will have a section to enable ReWire inputs. In Cubase this is under the Devices menu. A window opens that lets you activate and rename ReWire channels which correspond directly to the ports on Reason's hardware interface. Mix L and Mix R are the main stereo outputs from Reason's mixer. This is the simplest way to use ReWire, and means that the whole mix is streamed through on a stereo channel. A mixer in Reason will automatically be routed to channels 1 and 2 on the Hardware Interface, but there's nothing to stop you moving them to any other ports.

Things to remember when using ReWire

The host application always sets the master tempo. Altering the tempo in Reason will affect both programs, unless you are using automated tempo changes (a tempo track) in the host program. In this case, changing the tempo in Reason has no effect.

Though you can draw in tempo and time signature automation in the Transport sequencer track in Reason 4 and 5 when in ReWire mode, it won't have any effect. Only tempo and time signature automation in the master sequencer will work. When you're not in ReWire mode, the same automation data in Reason will work as normal.

Routing a stereo mix through from Reason is good, but means you can't process any Reason tracks individually in your host's mixer. It's better to start separating instruments off and assigning them to their own ReWire channels. This gives you much more flexibility.

You can assign MIDI tracks in your host sequencer to play Reason's instruments, without needing to have Reason in the foreground. The names of the instruments will appear in the list of available MIDI destinations on the MIDI track. You can set MIDI to be routed through from the host to Reason to play the track live, and also to assign existing MIDI tracks in the host to use Reason's instruments rather than their own virtual synths.

Figure 3.11
Reason's instruments are playable via MIDI tracks in the host sequencer.

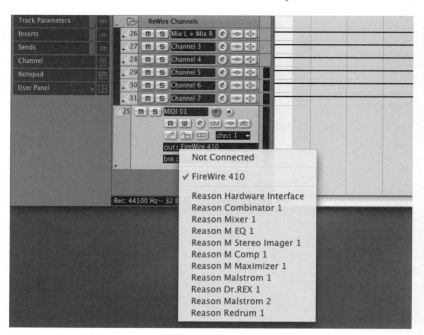

When you name instruments in Reason, either on the module or in the sequencer, that name is the one that is broadcast over ReWire. It's good practice to name things properly, or you end up with a list of ReDrum 1, ReDrum 2 and so on.

Converting ReWire to audio

Audio streamed into a host from Reason over ReWire is treated like any other audio channel. That is, you can apply effects and EQ to it. This means that

Figure 3.12
ReWire channels are included in audio mixdowns from the host sequencer.

you can use VST, Audio Unit, RTAS or DXi effects on Reason's instruments, which sort of gets around its not supporting external plugins. So in practice you may well be able to leave channels as ReWire, as they will be exported with any final mixdown from your host just as if they existed as audio within the host.

In some situations you may want to convert ReWire outputs to audio files. For example, to perform edits or special effects that are easier to achieve on an audio file than a MIDI file. You may also want to finish a project entirely in your host sequencer and not have to boot Reason up if the final arrangement is correct for the MIDI parts. The easiest way to turn ReWire into audio is to solo the relevant ReWire tracks in the host sequencer and bounce them down. In Cubase, the process would go something like this.

- Solo one or more ReWire tracks in the Cubase mixer. Choose only the ones you want to convert.
- Set the L and R locators over the section you need. Refer to Reason's sequencer here, as there will be no audio material in Cubase yet to show where to begin and end. Turn looping off.
- Select File > Audio Mixdown (or the equivalent in your sequencer).
- If there is an option, choose to import the newly created file onto a new audio track in the host sequencer. In Cubase this is Import to Audio track

Tip

Having ReWire channels activated uses processing power, so only activate as many as you're using. You can switch them on or off at any point.

Figure 3.13
You may have to render tracks out through the host sequencer, then bring them back in as audio files onto new tracks.

and Import to Pool. As the file is exported, any automation, EQ and effects applied in Cubase are included in the rendered file.

- The file is imported, so disable the ReWire channel you just rendered down, or the original will continue to play through from Reason.

If there is no auto-import option in your host's export dialogue box, make sure you know where the file is being saved to then use File > Import in the host to bring the rendered file back into the host project. It is also possible of course to export loops or tracks from Reason to your hard drive, then import them to the host in this way, without using ReWire. The disadvantage of this is that you have to be happy with the Reason tracks before you export them, as the notes will stop being editable. Many host DAWs support the 'freezing' of tracks, which invisibly renders them to audio to save CPU power.

If you also have Propellerheads' Record software, you can use all of Reason's modules automatically inside Record, and also record audio tracks in a much more conventional way. This turns Reason into part of a wider and more integrated production system, though neither application supports third-party plug-ins.

The Mixer

Reason's mixer works in much the same way as a real hardware mixer. If you have experience with real mixers it will make a lot of sense. If you don't, it's a good way to learn about how routing and mixing work. In all probability, everything you do in Reason will involve using at least one mixer.

A mixer has 14 channel strips, each with separate level, EQ, Pan, solo / mute and aux controls. Each channel is stereo, though to save space only a single LED meter is shown per channel. There's also a master fader and an effect return section. Each channel strip has a signal path, but it doesn't correspond to the physical order of the knobs on the channel.

Tip

As you create devices in the rack, they are automatically placed on the next available mixer channel. If you delete a device from the middle of the rack then create a new one, Reason will use the mixer channel that was just vacated, so you don't have to shuffle channels around.

Aux returns

The aux return section at the top right of the mixer is where you control the levels of the send effects that you attach to the mixer. When the mixer is selected (with a light blue outline around it) and you select Create and then

Figure 4.1
Reason's mixer.

an effect module, the effect is attached to the mixer as a send effect, and automatically routed to the next available aux channel. If you spin the rack around you will see Reason automatically patches send effects to the aux return section (Figure 4.2).

Figure 4.2
Effects created when the mixer is selected are automatically routed as sends.

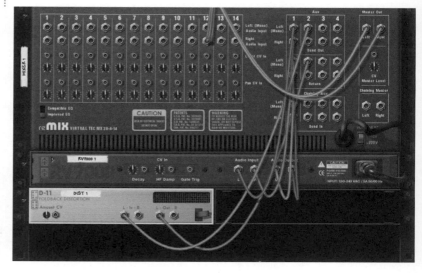

Send effects

In Reason, as in other sequencers and real hardware studios, effects can be applied in two main ways. As inserts or sends. Insert effects are attached between an instrument and the mixer, so the mixer receives signal that has already been effected. Send effects are attached to the mixer, and then become available to every channel on the mixer. In many situations you will want to have a few standard effects that are applied to every channel. Typically this might be a reverb, a compressor and a delay unit. Most of the tracks in your project may need a small amount of reverb on them. Applying a reverb unit to every instrument as an insert is both time consuming and power-hungry. Instead, add a reverb as a send effect and then by increasing the aux send for the channel that reverb is attached to, you apply reverb to the channel. Every channel in a mixer can share each of the four send effects. The trick is to make one setting on the unit itself, then use the aux send levels on the channels to set how much effect is applied to each channel. So for example, if channel 1 had its aux1 send set at 127 but channel 2 had it set to 10, both channels would be going through the same send effect, but channel 1 would have much more effect applied. By altering the aux return level on the mixer you can place a limit on the maximum effect level that will be applied. When you create a send effect its return level defaults to 100, which

Figure 4.3
Using effects as sends to conserve CPU. Vary the send amounts for each channel on the mixer.

is probably adequate for most uses. To get bigger effects you can raise this level to 127.

Many of the controls on the mixer are knobs. The best way to move them is to click and hold on them with the mouse, then drag straight up or down. The faster you drag, the more quickly the control will move. To get better control you can go into Reason's preferences and set General > Mouse Knob Range to Very Precise. Alternatively for less specific control, set it to Normal. If you hold down the shift key as you drag the knobs, they move in much smaller increments, which can be useful, especially when automating them.

Figure 4.4
Setting the mouse knob sensitivity.

Info

By using effects as sends you reduce the CPU requirements of a project. Ten channels going through one reverb send effect use a lot less power than ten reverbs applied as inserts.

The Master Fader

The master fader controls the master output of all channels in the mixer. Every channel is sent to it and then a single mixed signal is sent on, usually to the Hardware Interface. It's important to keep an eye on the master fader when mixing, as sometimes when you think the track doesn't seem loud enough, it's because the master fader is set too low. The master fader is where you can control master fade ins and fade outs for your tracks.

Figure 4.5
The master fader – small but important.

Why are my tracks so quiet?

A common mistake is to boost all the channels up to maximum to try to make them louder. Channels shouldn't be competing with each other – the concept of mixing is to achieve a balance of sounds. The master fader defaults to a volume level of 100, and this is a good level to work with. You can push it higher, as long as the level meters don't stay at the very top. You can go lower, but if you go too low you'll need to boost your monitoring system just to hear the track, and you'll probably also start getting hiss in the sound. If your tracks seem too quiet there are some things to check.

Figure 4.6
Keep an eye on the master level

- Look if the master fader is set to between 90 and 110. These are good levels to work with in general. Your guide should be the coloured LED meters. They should be well into the orange during louder sections of music, but not consistently hitting the top.
- The Audio Out Clipping indicator at the bottom left of the transport panel will light up if your overall signal is too high. Lower the master fader to correct this.
- You shouldn't really be running audio channels with the faders jammed

Figure 4.7
Every instrument and most effects have
a separate master volume control.

right to the top. If the faders are nearly at full stretch and it's still not
loud enough, go to the instrument itself and raise the Master Level
control on it. Every instrument has a master volume control and not all
default to full volume.

- If an effect is applied as an insert, check that its master volume level is
  turned up far enough, and that the effect you're applying isn't limiting
  the volume of the sound passing through it. Some effects like EQ and
  reverb used heavily can have the unintentional effect of quietening the
  signal.
- If you are running in ReWire mode, be sure to check that the channels
  running through to the other sequencer are turned up, and that effects
  applied in that sequencer aren't limiting the volume.
- Remember your external hardware. If you are running instruments
  directly out to a real mixer, check the channel and master faders on that
  mixer.
- Make sure your speakers are turned up. This sounds simplistic, but it's
  very easy to be baffled by a quiet signal when everything looks OK, only
  to realise your speakers are set to low volume. Also look at your
  soundcard's control panel to ensure the outputs you're using are
  switched up properly.

Tips for mixing music

There are some good general rules for mixing regardless of platform or software. The process of mixing a track always involves some common elements
such as setting levels, setting EQ and adding effects and fades. Mixing is fairly subjective, although a 'bad' mix will probably sound bad to everyone who
hears it. A good mix means people probably won't notice the work that's
gone into getting it right, because by definition it should just sound 'right'.
A great mix will probably only be fully appreciated by music types, although
it should still be your aim! Here are some things you should remember when
mixing tracks.

- Take a mixdown of your track as a WAV or AIFF file, burn it to CD and
  listen to it on a number of different music systems. It might sound good
  on your expensive monitors, but not on your friend's hi-fi. Try playing it
  through a range of systems from high-end equipment to car stereos and
  personal CD players. By doing this, any problems with the mix will
  become evident. For example, the bass might sound right on your
  monitors, but be nonexistent on a smaller system. Changing the mix and

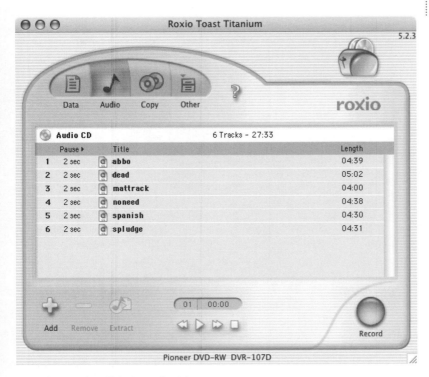

Figure 4.8
Burn a CD of your mix and try it on other systems.

trying again will help to fix this.

- Work with a decent soundcard and a decent monitoring system. A pair of old hi-fi speakers is OK but won't help you get the best possible mix.
- Don't decide on a final mix when you've been listening to the same track all day. Your ears get tired and it becomes hard to judge what sounds right and wrong. Take an hour or two off, or better still, leave it a day or two and come back with a fresh perspective.
- Get a second opinion. If you're working on your own, ask someone whose opinion you value to listen to the mix. Having not heard it a thousand times, they may well have some useful suggestions that you wouldn't otherwise have thought of.
- Don't mix at loud volumes. By all means turn it up a couple of times to see how the mix holds up, but constant loud monitoring won't give a true picture of how the track sounds.
- If you're doing an album, make sure all the tracks sound like they belong on the same record. That is, they are all mixed to about the same level.

Chaining mixers

Reason's modular structure means that everything can be freely patched. One result of this is that you aren't limited to having one mixer in a project. After all, if you could only have 14 channels you would run out of options fairly quickly. If you fill up your first mixer, create another one. Regardless of where it sits in the rack, Reason will know it's a mixer and connect it to the chaining inputs on the first mixer. Any instruments you create after this should be routed to the second mixer, and the mixer's master outputs will be sent back to the first mixer. It doesn't need a channel to be available on the

Figure 4.9
Chained mixers seen from the front...

Figure 4.10
...and from the back.

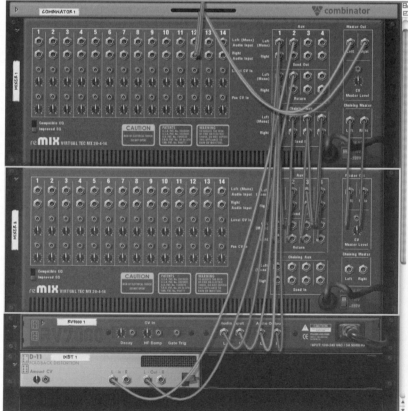

first mixer, as chaining is handled through a special set of connections. When you've filled up the first mixer, make sure that you select the second mixer when creating further instruments, otherwise the new instruments won't be auto-routed. Alternatively, make sure that you have a module below the second mixer in the rack selected when creating new instruments. That way, Reason knows to connect them to the second mixer. Of course you can spin the rack around and patch the instruments yourself if you like. When mixers are chained their aux sends are connected to the chaining aux inputs on the first mixer. This means that all channels in the second mixer can access the send effects connected to the first mixer. If you only need a few more channels you can use a Line mixer instead.

Remember that although a lot of patching happens automatically, you can change it if you like. For example, you can disconnect the aux sends from the second mixer and then attach up to four effects to that mixer, using them as independent sends, available only to the channels on that mixer. Although subsequent mixers are connected automatically to the previous mixer via the chaining bus, you can of course disconnect them and route them through to separate channels on the Hardware Interface. You can create as many mixers as your system will run, so in theory you can have, say, ten mixers all connected to channels on the Hardware Interface and all outputting to separate ports on your soundcard. One application for this might be if you were making tracks with a lot of instruments, you could have a mixer for each group of sounds. One for the drums, one for the basses, the synths and so on. The other great thing about chaining mixers is that it gets around the problem of only having four send effect slots.

Figure 4.11
A complex example of routing multiple mixers straight to the Hardware Interface.

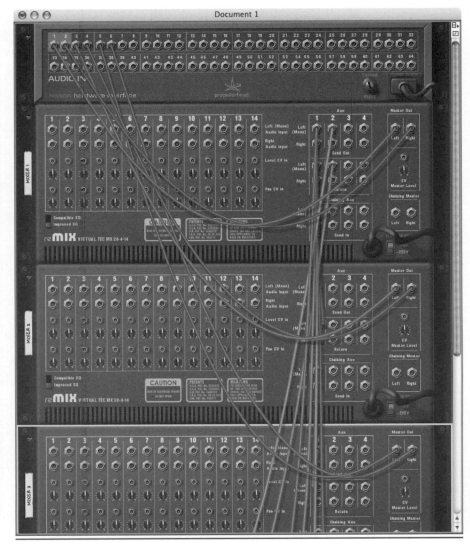

Figure 4.12
Names set on the instrument will also
update on the mixer.

Figure 4.14
Use the EQ controls to help sounds sit
better in the mix.

The Channel Strip

Each channel strip has some common elements. Here are some tips for using
and being creative with mixer channels.

The channel names are read-only, but if you edit the name of an instrument or module, it is updated on the mixer channel that module is connected to. Get into the habit of naming modules as you create them. Otherwise
you tend to end up with Dr:Rex 1, Dr:Rex 2 and so on, which is tiresome
when you have to mute or solo channels and you don't know what's playing
through what. Even just naming the modules after the instrument you load
into them will make your life easier.

When you solo a channel, all other channels will be muted. You can solo
other channels to bring them back into the mix. When you mute a channel,
that channel alone is muted. Further channels can be independently muted
to knock them out of the mix. If you have multiple mixers, solo and mute only
affect the mixer you click on, so any channels on other mixers will need to be
sooled or muted separately. As of Reason 3, the sequencer also has proper
solo and mute controls.

Figure 4.13
Solo and mute
individual channels.

Using the pan control will help you to achieve more interesting mixes.
Most records use panning to create stereo effects. For example, if you duplicate a device in the rack, connect it to the next mixer channel and duplicate
its sequencer track, then pan one channel hard left and one hard right, you'll
get a fuller sound from the instrument. Two instances of it will be playing at
once using exactly the same notes. Label the first instrument something like
Piano L and the second Piano R.

Blending sounds into a mix is often best achieved by using EQ. By pressing the EQ button to activate it for a channel, you can raise or lower the tre-
ble and bass of that channel until it sits better in the mix. Reason 2.5 has
two EQ modes. Look on the back of the mixer and a switch lets you toggle
between Compatible and Improved EQ modes. If you are opening songs created in an old version of Reason you can use Compatible mode to make sure
they play back identically to the old version. Generally though you'll want to
leave this on the Improved setting.

The Aux send controls let you vary the amount of signal that is sent to the
send effects. If you press the P button, pre-fader mode is activated for aux send
4. This means that the send effects is applied after the EQ and pan controls but

Figure 4.15
Automating mixer controls.

before the signal reaches the fader. This allows you to lower the fader completely and just hear the wet signal as passed through send effect 4.

All the controls on a mixer can be automated. If you hold down the alt key when clicking on a mixer control, the sequencer window will jump to edit view and display the automation timeline for that control. As a lot of automation is fine tuned using pen tools in edit mode, this is a quick way of tweaking automation without having to click through several menus. See chapter 6 for tips on automation in Reason.

The Line Mixer

Reason has a mini-mixer called the 6:2 Line mixer. Its six stereo input channels are combined to a single master stereo out, which is then sent on to the main mixer or to a Combinator or other device. It has several uses. Here are some suggestions.

The Line Mixer is ideal for sub-mixing devices, especially within a Combinator patch. All the devices in a Combinator must have their outputs collected together to form a stereo output to be sent onwards to the mixer. If you create a Combinator and add devices to it one by one, only the first

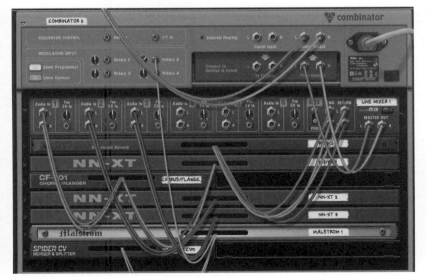

Figure 4.16
The Line mixer is ideal for submixing devices within a combi.

Info

Each of the six channels has level, mute, solo, pan and an aux send, so you can fine-tune the mixture of sounds within a Combi before it ever reaches the main mixer.

Tip

If you use the Line Mixer in a Combi or on its own in the rack, it can be used just to create supplementary send effects to add to the four allowed by the ReMix.

instrument will be auto-routed. If you create a Line mixer and then add the instruments, they will be properly routed and when you play a note, all instruments will be triggered.

This mixer is best to use when you need to mix a few devices together, and when a full ReMix would be overkill. You can of course have any number of Line Mixers within a Combi or within the rack itself. You can manually patch any modules through a Line Mixer – it doesn't have to happen within a Combinator.

You can attach a send effect to a Line mixer and it can be controlled using the aux send and return controls. Each of the six channels can have independent amounts of the send applied. If you create a send chain, by adding a few send effects one after the other, the effects are applied together. In this way you can build up huge effects within a Combi.

Figure 4.17
A send effect connected to a Line mixer.

The Sequencer

Virtual instruments are nothing without a sequencer to tell them what to play. MIDI notes are played into the sequencer, and the sequencer tracks are connected to instruments, which then output sound. As well as simple notes, the sequencer in Reason is where you control all automation and pattern data. Sequencing implies building up a track from different parts, and as well as editing notes, the sequencer is where you assemble groups of notes into whole tracks. There are two main modes in Reason – Arrange and Edit. Arrange is where you build the track and see it graphically as layers of notes. Edit is where you view and change all the parameters of an instrument or a pattern.

Figure 5.1
Toggle between Arrange and Edit modes.

Sequencer basics

Every instrument in the rack must have a sequencer track associated with it if it is to play notes back. The instrument that you play from the MIDI keyboard is the one with a small keyboard displayed underneath its icon when its sequencer track is selected. A green level meter which jumps when you hit a key means that MIDI is being routed to that instrument. Click in this area on another sequencer track to send MIDI to it.

As of Reason 3, multiple MIDI devices can be used at the same time. It's a good idea to have one Master keyboard which directs MIDI to whichever module you select, and have subsequent controllers locked to specific devices in the rack.

In Reason 3 you can change the instrument associated with a sequencer track at any point by clicking the arrow next to its name and selecting from the list of available modules. This is useful if you want to

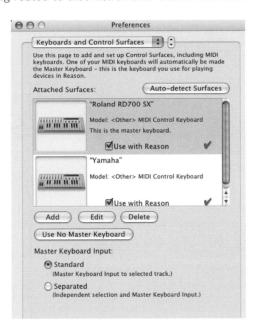

Figure 5.2
Specify a master keyboard, which will always be playable, in the preferences.

51

Figure 5.3
Manually redirect MIDI for a sequencer track to a different instrument in Reason 3 but NOT in Reason 4 or 5.

see how a melody will sound played using a different instrument, but don't want to re-play or copy and paste the notes. In Reason 4 and 5 the sequencer is revamped and you must create a new device first since sequencer tracks now have multiple lanes, often specific to a device.

As you add more and more tracks, use the zoom controls to the left and right of the sequencer to get a better view. Also, use the small click box at the top right of the sequencer to maximise or minimize it.

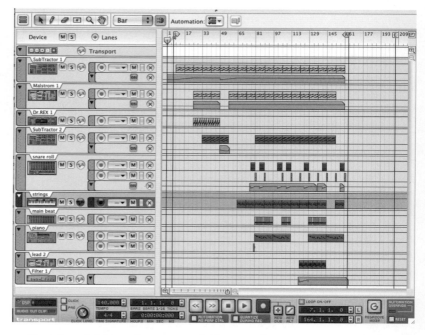

Figure 5.4
Zoom out horizontally and vertically to get a better overall view of bigger projects.

The left and right markers are crucial for recording loops and exporting material. Use alt + click on the timeline to set the position of the left marker and apple + click (Mac) or control + click (PC) to set the right. Alternatively, drag them to the desired position or enter position values in the toolbar.

Working with sequencer tracks

Material in the sequencer can be used in different ways. By material, we mean MIDI information. This can take the form of notes or other controller data such as velocity, sustain or automation. You can import MIDI files using the File > Import command as well as playing MIDI in yourself. Data on sequencer tracks displays in Arrange view as small black dots and if you zoom in you can see their positions reflect where they sit on the scale. Reason 4 now works with clips, which are essentially groups of notes or data. These are created automatically when you record and can be shortened or lengthened by dragging their edges.

Tip

By shift + clicking on the timeline you can set the end point of the project, which is displayed as a marker labeled E. To lengthen or shorten a project, pick up this marker and drag it to the right or left.

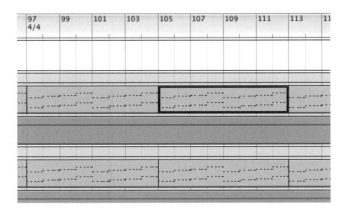

Figure 5.5
Reason automatically creates clips when recording notes.

Elements of the Sequencer

Views

Key Edit

When you are in Edit mode (toggle using the button at the top left of the Sequencer) there are various different views that you can use. The most common is called the Key Lane. This simply displays the notes you have played as data, along with a keyboard for reference. This is where you perform detailed editing of MIDI notes. When you select a note it goes darker and gains a black dot to its right. Picking this dot up and dragging it will extend the length of the note. Notes can be dragged anywhere on a key editor to change the note that is played back. If you hold down alt (Mac) or Control (PC) and drag a note or group of notes they are duplicated. By drawing round groups of notes you can multiple select them and move them all together. Pressing backspace or selecting Edit > Delete or Cut will get rid of the notes.

Tip

To make an instrument play exactly the same notes as another instrument, simply copy the notes from one sequencer track to the other.

Tip

With a group of notes selected, if you lengthen or shorten one note, all the others will be altered by the same amount.

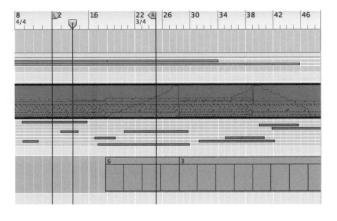

Figure 5.6
Reason can be set to auto colour new sequencer tracks to make identifying clips easier.

Figure 5.7
Reason colour codes clips in the Sequencer.

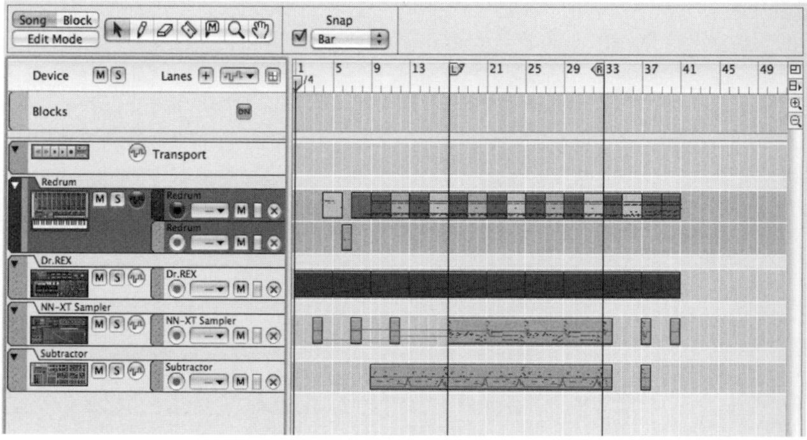

Tip

In Key Edit mode, if you move the mouse over the vertical keyboard display the cursor changes to a tiny speaker. You can then play any of the notes using the mouse, to audition the sound without having to go to your MIDI keyboard.

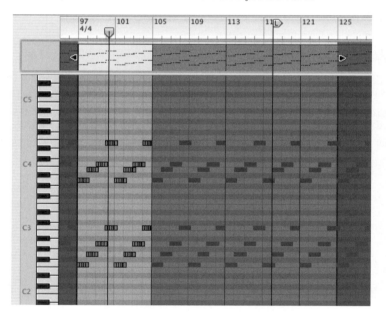

In Edit mode, if you select different tracks from the track list on the left, the edit view on the right changes to display the notes for that track. If the track has additional types of control going on – say, patterns for a ReDrum or automation, those will automatically be displayed, meaning you don't have to switch different views on and off to see what a track contains. If you customise a view for a specific track, it is remembered for the next time you look at it.

Figure 5.8
The Key Editor.

Info

The Hand tool can be used to scroll up or down and left to right in any editor.

Info

Reason now has a Razor tool which is used to make cuts over multiple sequencer lanes and then you can move the cut sections en masse with the pointer tool

Info

The Eraser tool, unsurprisingly, erases whatever note or data you touch with it.

REX Lane Edit

The Dr.Rex player, ReDrum, NN-19 and NN-XT all support the playback of REX files to differing extents. Whenever a REX loop is loaded, it becomes available to edit in the REX lane. It also remains editable in the Key Editor. Activating Show REX Lane gives you access to the individual slices. The slices are numbered, and the longer a loop, the more slices it will have. If you have created your own REX files using ReCycle these numbers will correspond to the number of slices you chose.

The Key Editor and REX Lane editor should display the same patterns. This is because a REX file consists of slices of audio triggered by MIDI. Each note corresponds to a MIDI note on your keyboard and so slices 1 to 30 for example will equate to notes C1 up to almost C3 on the keyboard. If you have both open at the same time you can see that moving a note in one will affect the other. However, the loops (or groups of notes) exist independently on the timeline. If you change one, the others remain the same. This is useful for creating variations in REX loops without worrying about changing every loop.

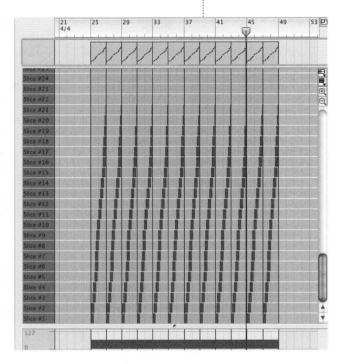

Figure 5.9
The REX lane displays REX loop information.

Drum Edit

Any ReDrum will have a Drum Edit lane available. This corresponds to each of the channels on the ReDrum, and the names of the loaded samples are displayed in the lane. Like with the Key Editor, you can audition any of these samples by clicking on their name in the edit lane.

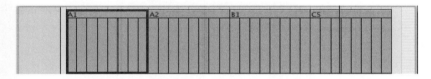

Figure 5.10
The ReDrum works with patterns as well as notes, via the Pattern lane.

The ReDrum is a bit different because it's a pattern device. This means you don't have to enter notes in the Drum or Key editors if you don't want to. By using Step Input mode and the pattern lane, you can sequence drums without playing MIDI keys. See the ReDrum chapter for more on this. The same applies to the Kong device.

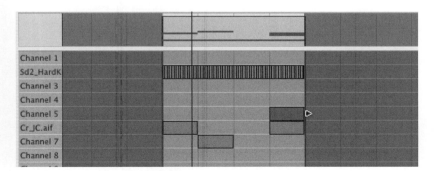

Figure 5.11
The Drum lane, where note data is shown in the same way as the other instruments.

You can of course enter drum data the traditional way, by simply playing it in from a MIDI keyboard. In this case, notes appear in the Drum Editor and the Key Editor and can be manipulated in the same way as any other notes.

Velocity Lane

Every note has a velocity value, determining how loud it is. These range from zero to 127 – not actual decibels, but MIDI values. You can see the velocity of notes by activating the Velocity Lane, which should appear by default anyway. The darker the shade of red, the higher the velocity.

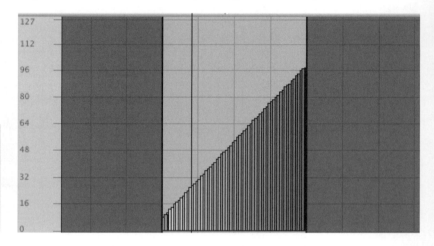

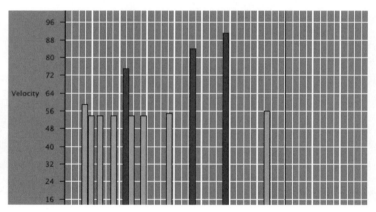

Use the pencil tool to edit the velocity of individual notes. Click above or below a note in the velocity lane to change the value. To create gradual changes, draw from one side to the other whilst also going up or down. Click and drag in the Velocity lane to create uniform changes. This is particularly useful for creating drum rolls as well as evening out natural variations in your playing which you may not want to be present.

Figure 5.12
Create velocity ramps and edit velocity data in the Velocity lane.

Figure 5.13
Edit nonsequential notes' values by using key presses when editing them.

If you multiple select notes and then hold down Shift when editing velocity values, only the notes you have selected will be affected. This is useful in places where there are many notes crowded together and you only want to edit certain ones by the same amount. For example, in a drum pattern let's say you wanted to make every other snare hit louder. Changing volume on the ReDrum would change every snare hit. Selecting every other beat in the velocity editor then using shift and the line tool would save you a lot of time.

Pattern Lane

Any pattern device like the ReDrum or Matrix can store a number of preset patterns, which can then be triggered at different points from the Sequencer. The Pattern Lane works not with MIDI notes but blocks which determine which sequence is played, and for how long. For more information on this see the Matrix section below, and the ReDrum chapter.

Tip

To delete a pattern automation clip simply select it and hit backspace.

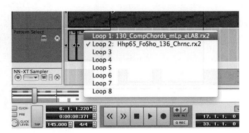

Figure 5.14
The Pattern lane.

Controllers

Almost every parameter on every module can be controlled and automated. Parameter changes range from simple on / off controls to filter sweeps, effects amounts, LFO controls and so on. This is usually achieved by creating a sequencer track for the device (if it doesn't already have one) and then changing the parameters in realtime as you play and record. In Reason, automation can be recorded on multiple tracks at the same time. Simply activate the red record button (Record Enable Parameter Automation) next to each track in the sequencer you want to automate. Obviously this works better it you have multiple MIDI control devices plugged in, as you can only do so much at once with the mouse.

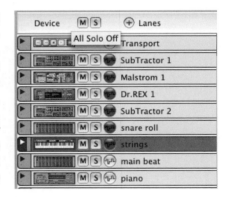

Figure 5.15
Record automation on multiple channels at once.

To record multiple automation parameters using just the mouse, set up a loop over the section of music you want and use the red buttons to automation-enable the desired devices. Then as you play back and loop you can move between devices and alter parameters. Everything you have previously automated will continue to play back that automation as you record new changes in realtime, all without having to stop recording.

With so many parameters available for automation, a quick way of specifying one to view in edit mode is to hold Option (Mac) or Alt (PC) and click on it. This opens edit view and brings the automation subtrack for that parameter to the front. It also adds an automation sub-lane to that sequencer track and activates it. This saves a lot of time hunting for the relevant subtrack, especially if many are automated. This can also be done by Control

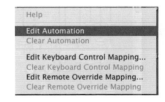

Figure 5.16
Quickly jump to the automation subtrack for any available control.

(Mac) or right-clicking (PC) on a parameter and choosing Edit Automation from the contextual menu.

> **Info**
>
> **R**ight click on a sequencer track and choose Parameter Automation. Then from the resulting window, choose which available parameters are shown in the automation lanes for that device.

> **Info**
>
> **A**utomation data in controller subtracks is edited using the Pen tool, with which it can be drawn in. Holding down Shift when using the Line tool restricts it to horizontal values only, useful for ensuring constant settings.

In Reason 3 it is possible to copy and paste automation between controller lanes in the Sequencer, for the same track or different tracks. This works using the usual copy or cut and then paste, when you have selected the target subtrack. This also works with multiple parameters using Shift to multiple select areas of data. Automation data can be dragged around the sub-track to move it. Rather than try-ing to recreate the same sweep or fade, just copy the automation from the subtrack. You can select it and then use Alt (Mac) or Control (PC) and drag to duplicate it. Automation in Reason 4 and 5 works in a different way. See Chapter 6 for more on this.

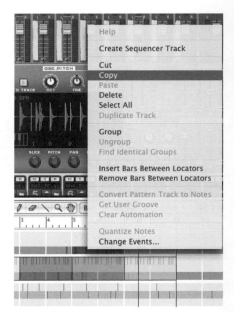

Figure 5.17
Copy and paste automation between tracks in Reason 3.

The Sequencer in Reason 4 and 5

The sequencer in Reason 4 had had a major overhaul and is now slightly more complex but much more powerful than before, and still easy to use. It's much the same in Reason 5 as in 4. Here's how it works.

Instead of basic notes, Reason now uses lanes, clips and events. A device in the rack has a single track but that track can have many lanes – think of them as sub-tracks containing data and connected to that device. At its most basic a device might have a single lane containing note data. Or if there is some automation or sustain pedal data associated with that track, it will appear on a new lane underneath the first note lane. Additional lanes can be added using the plus arrow, and deleted using the x button on each lane. They can be muted by turning off their On button. Lanes for automation data can be shown by choosing available parameters from the Automation drop-down menu on the main toolbar.

As well as automation data or controllers, lanes can hold regular notes. You can add a note lane using the plus arrow at the top of the track list and

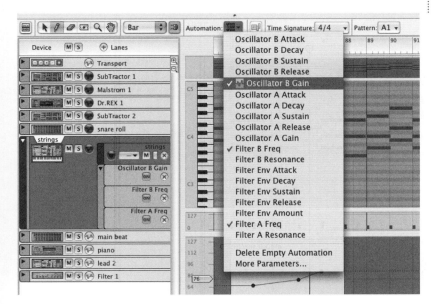

Figure 5.18
The automation dropdown menu and some automation lanes.

then record or drag a new clip onto it, containing notes (also referred to as 'events'). This means you can have quite complex parts all running through the same device without clogging up a single sequencer track and thus being difficult to see or edit.

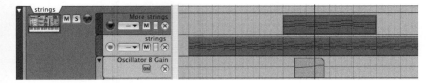

Figure 5.19
Multiple note parts on a single sequencer track using lanes.

A great use for lanes is to keep different elements of a loop on separate lanes in order to have better control over them. A typical example might involve a drum kit, and recording the kick onto one lane, the snare onto another, ride cymbal on another and so on until you have a layered MIDI part. Each of these can then be routed individually to a ReGroove mixer channel, meaning you can give each part of the kit its own specific groove, shuffle and timing. No longer are you limited to quantizing a whole drum part as one. To facilitate this 'stacked' recording, there are two new buttons on the Transport. New Dub, when pressed, creates a new lane on the fly so you can overdub further notes in a loop. New Alt does the same but mutes the previous takes so you can have a fresh canvas to try another go – all without stopping playback or recording.

Clips have replaced the old Groups in previous versions of Reason and are created automatically when you record. They can also be drawn in using the pen tool. Clips can be muted by selecting them and pressing M and you can also add labels to them which is extremely useful. Clips can be coloured, joined, cropped and their groove extracted, all via a simple right click on a clip.

> **Tip**
>
> Show and hide automation channels by clicking their expand / collapse arrow.

> **Tip**
>
> You can multiple select tracks by shift or option clicking on them.

Figure 5.20
Clip operations in the sequencer.

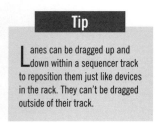

Tip

Lanes can be dragged up and down within a sequencer track to reposition them just like devices in the rack. They can't be dragged outside of their track.

Figure 5.21
Clips display the notes within them, if you look closely.

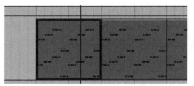

Figure 5.22
Use the Tool window to quickly access note editing functions.

Info

If you have several note lanes on a track and want to merge them into a single lane whilst maintaining the independence of the clips, right click or from the Edit menu choose Merge Note Lanes on Tracks. Automation lanes remain unaffected.

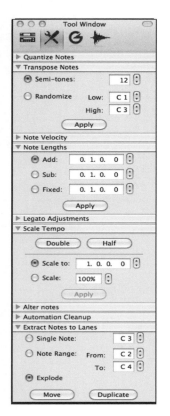

Time signature and tempo can now be automated. See Chapter 6 for more on this, and many operations on note clips in the sequencer can now be performed quickly and easily from the Tools section of the Tool window.

What are Blocks?

Blocks are a new way to compose and sequence material in addition to the more conventional, linear technique that Reason has used since its creation. The concept is a little bit like song sequencing in old hardware sequencers and drum machines. Essentially, if you enter Blocks mode you can compose short sections of music using any of the instrument modules in the sequencer. So for example you might build an intro, verse, chorus, breakdown and an outro in a series of blocks. Then back in Song mode you draw in a sequence of blocks in order to create your song structure. It's like 'painting' in parts of a song.

Working with Blocks

You can move the Blocks around in Song mode and change their assignment, quickly replacing a breakdown with another instance of the verse, for example. This is done by simply clicking on one and changing the Block to which it refers, just like you do when automating patterns elsewhere in Reason.

When you have entered Blocks in Song mode, the MIDI clips associated with the blocks are displayed in the sequencer but they are 'ghosted', meaning displayed quite faintly. You can use the new Mute tool to quickly mute

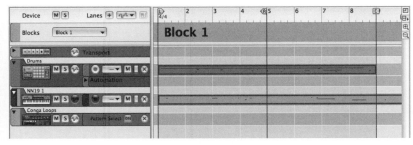

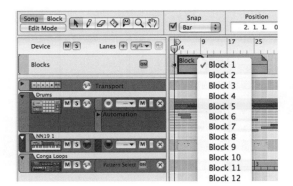

Figure 5.23
Blocks mode is a new way to compose in Reason 5.

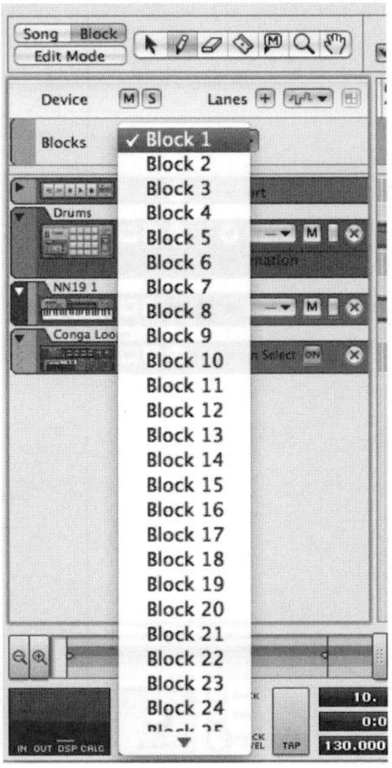

Figure 5.24
Quickly select a Block to work on when in Blocks mode.

blocks, altering an arrangement on the fly. You can also make a block 'real' by choosing to convert it to song clips, at which point the MIDI clips it contains are transferred into the main Sequencer and can be freely edited in Song mode. Do this by right clicking on a Block and choosing the relevant option. If however you want to make a project-wide change to a block, you can edit it in Blocks mode and the change will update wherever that block exists in the project. Since the blocks of data in Song mode are referencing the MIDI in the block, then as long as a block has not been converted to a Song clip this trick will work.

Figure 5.25
Reassign a Block from Song mode to change the arrangement.

Tips for working with Blocks

A useful trick to know is that new parts can be added to a sequencer track even if it contains blocks of data. Let's say that in the lead up to a drum part you wanted to add a couple of extra drum hits, but only once and not for every instance of that block. Simply locate the MIDI part in Song mode and record the new part. MIDI recorded in Song mode takes precedence over that contained in a block, so it's easy to add new parts and embellishments.

Blocks have many potential uses, whatever kind of music you are working with. Perhaps the most obvious is for electronic music, with blocks being the simplest way of creating buildups, dropouts and other sections and then linking them together to make a song. As it's so easy to shorten, lengthen or reassign a block, playing with the length and structure of a track is very quick with little or no copying and pasting of large amounts of data around the sequencer.

For more conventional songwriting, you could use blocks to quickly paint in a backing track of drums and bass while you improvised or composed over the top. The two sequencing methods can be used separately or together for ultimate flexibility.

Info

It's important to understand the relationship between Block mode and Song mode. In Block mode you work on individual sections of music, but you can create and edit parts for every module loaded in the rack. Blocks can be of different lengths, you just have to drag the End marker within the Block. In Song mode you can paint in Blocks of music but still edit and overdub new notes, so the two are not mutually exclusive.

Recording data inside Blocks works in exactly the same way as it does in the main Sequencer. Tracks accept MIDI input and data can be edited, quantized and generally messed about with. You can record multiple clips on multiple tracks within a Block, making them almost like miniature songs within a song. They can be as simple or as complex as you like.

You can work with a maximum of 32 Blocks in any one project. If this isn't enough, choose some Blocks and convert them to Song clips, freeing up that block for re-use. You can also re-use the same Block several times but then selectively mute certain tracks or lanes within a Block in the sequencer to make it different from other instances of the same Block.

Performance controller and automation data in Song view always overrides automation data contained in a Block.

If you right click on a Block in Song mode you can choose to create a pattern / loop lane for the currently selected instrument in the Sequencer. This lets you quickly jump to recording pattern changes for a device that allows them such as Kong, the ReDrum or the RPG-8.

Tip

The quickest way to move data between Blocks, say to create a new one based on the existing one, is to use the standard copy and paste commands, with the part or parts selected in Block mode.

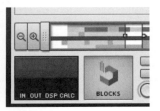

Figure 5.26
Quickly enable or disable Blocks mode with the button on the Transport panel.

Tip

"Ghosted" data can exist in the sequencer at the same time as a "real" MIDI clip. However data in Song clips – in the main sequencer – takes priority over ghosted data from a Block. This is a good way to quickly overdub the content of a track within a Block without affecting other instances of that Block.

Figure 5.27
Enter Blocks mode then hit the Edit button to edit a part in its respective Edit view inside the Block.

Info

You can rename blocks by double clicking on their names to make the name field editable in Blocks mode. This is a really good idea since it will help you to structure your tracks. If Blocks are called things like "intro", "verse" and "chorus" instead of 1, 2 and 3, it makes things much easier to manage.

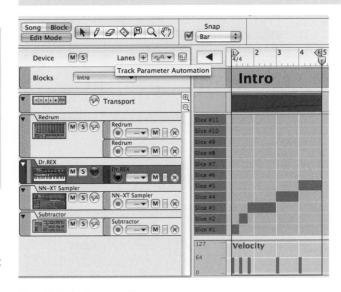

The Matrix Pattern Sequencer

The Matrix pattern sequencer is sometimes overlooked but is actually a very powerful tool that complements Reason's main sequencer. The best way to think of it is as a sort of step sequencer – similar to old hardware sequencers like Roland Grooveboxes. It doesn't generate sound, but sends CV (control voltage) signal to CV inputs on other modules. It can transmit three types of CV data:

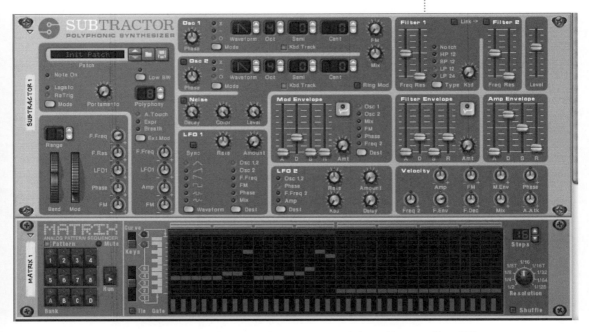

Figure 5.28
The Matrix is ideal for creating sequences of notes for electronic music.

- Note CV, which controls the pitch of a note. The main part of the grid on a Matrix is for entering note data.
- Gate CV, which controls note on/off and level. This is important because without a note on and level value, a pitch value won't produce any sound. You need to tell a Matrix what note to play, at what level and for how long. The lower part of the grid is for entering gate CV.
- Curve CV, which is a more generic type of controller data to modulate other parameters such as filter, volume and pan.

The reason that the Matrix is so flexible is that it can control more or less any parameter. Most instruments and effects have a number of CV inputs to control different settings. Many also have sequencer control CV inputs. This is probably the most common use for a Matrix – to build up sequences of notes. Reason lends itself to electronic and dance music, so you may want to create

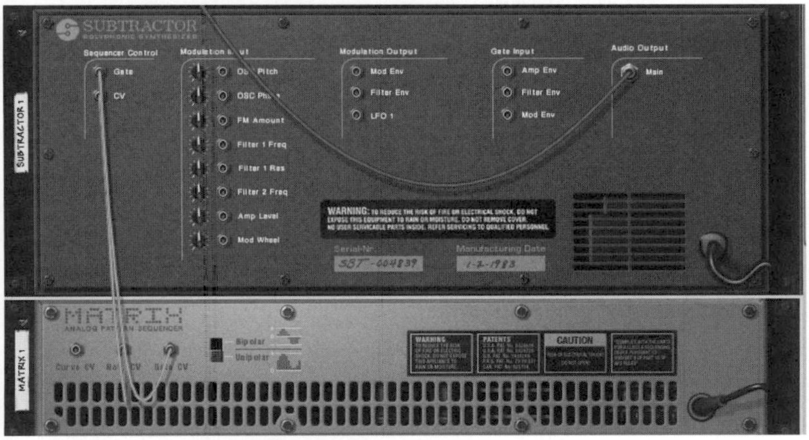

Figure 5.29
Connect a Matrix as you would connect an insert effect, and its note and gate CV outputs are automatically connected.≥

Figure 5.30
The Run button plays the Matrix independently of the main sequencer

Figure 5.31
The Resolution switch.

Figure 5.32
The Shuffle controls.

Figure 5.33 (right)
Create further variation in your sequences by connecting the curve CV output to the OSC pitch CV input on a synth.

acid or techno synth sequences. As the program lacks a dedicated arpeggiator module, you can use the Matrix to achieve complex patterns without having to play them in by hand.

Working with the Matrix

If you select an instrument in the rack and then create a Matrix, it will automatically be routed to the sequencer control inputs of that instrument. If the module does not have these inputs, the Matrix will remain unconnected until you patch it manually.

The Matrix can play independently of the main sequencer using its Run button. You can audition patterns without having to render them to the timeline. They remain 'virtual' within the Matrix. You can store up to 32 patterns in each Matrix sequencer. There are eight pattern slots and four banks. Switching between patterns is synchronized so the next one won't start playing until the last one has finished. This means no unexpected jumps.

Each of the 32 patterns stored can be completely different. Each can have a different length, resolution and octave setting. Each Matrix can only control a single voice in an instrument, but there's no limit to how many matrix modules you can create. Use the octave control on the left to move up and down the scale. A Matrix will always follow the master project tempo, but you can alter the resolution of the pattern using the knob on the right. Typically this might be 1/16.

To add swing to a pattern and make it feel less mechanical, activate the shuffle button on the Matrix. Set the amount of shuffle globally using the Pattern Shuffle knob on the Transport Panel. Shuffle on/off is stored separately with each pattern, so it can be on or off for any of the 32 patterns in a Matrix.

If you plug the outputs of a Matrix sequencer into other CV inputs such as filter, mod or pitch you can start to get some interesting sounds. For

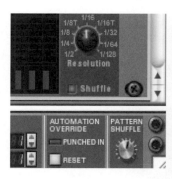
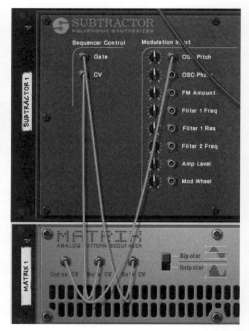

example, creating a sequence then connecting the Matrix to the OSC pitch and phase inputs on a Subtractor, then pressing Run on the Matrix and playing a MIDI note will produce a totally new sound.

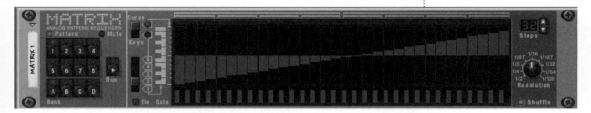

Following from the above example, if you switch from key to curve mode on the Matrix and connect the curve CV output to, say, the filter res input on the synth, you start to further affect the sound. A switch on the back of the Matrix lets you toggle between unipolar and bipolar modes. When drawing curve CV values, sometimes you need to go from plus into negative values. For example, when automating pan on the mixer. Fully to the top might represent a pan hard left and to the bottom, a pan hard right. In bipolar mode the centre line becomes zero. In unipolar mode the bottom line is zero.

Figure 5.34
Draw curve values by entering curve mode on the Matrix.

Tip

Part of the fun of sequences is adding an element of randomization. With a pattern selected in a Matrix, you can choose from the Edit menu to shift a pattern around, alter it or randomize it completely. Also use this menu to cut, paste and clear patterns.

Info

The Spider CV Merger / Splitter can take CV signal generated by a Matrix and send it to multiple destinations, or combine CV signal from several places. Practical applications for this include having a single Matrix play the same pattern on several synths at once, or automating filters on a number of devices at the same time, in perfect sync.

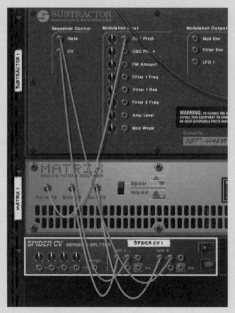

Figure 5.35
The Spider CV unit is the perfect partner for the Matrix

Tip

When drawing data into the note or curve CV grids, hold down shift to draw smooth, gradual values.

Tip

When drawing in gate CV in the lower part of the grid, hold the shift key to create tied rather than single notes. To permanently enable tied notes, press the Tie button. Now, pressing shift when drawing will enter single notes.

Tip

Each pattern can be between 1 and 32 steps long. To quickly alter this value, click and hold on the step box at the top right, then drag the mouse up or down.

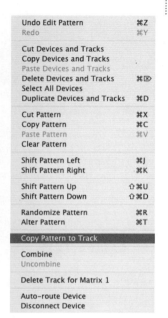

Undo Edit Pattern	⌘Z
Redo	⌘Y
Cut Devices and Tracks	
Copy Devices and Tracks	
Paste Devices and Tracks	
Delete Devices and Tracks	⌘⌦
Select All Devices	
Duplicate Devices and Tracks	⌘D
Cut Pattern	⌘X
Copy Pattern	⌘C
Paste Pattern	⌘V
Clear Pattern	
Shift Pattern Left	⌘J
Shift Pattern Right	⌘K
Shift Pattern Up	⇧⌘U
Shift Pattern Down	⇧⌘D
Randomize Pattern	⌘R
Alter Pattern	⌘T
Copy Pattern to Track	
Combine	
Uncombine	
Delete Track for Matrix 1	
Auto-route Device	
Disconnect Device	

Figure 5.36
Copying Matrix patterns to sequencer note data.

Figure 5.37
Dragging the Matrix notes to a module's sequencer track to make it play the same sequence of notes.

Figure 5.38
Recording pattern changes in realtime.

Recording Matrix data to sequencer tracks

After setting up all these different patterns, you do of course have to get them into the main sequencer in some way so Reason knows how to incorporate them into your track. There are several ways to do this, depending on how you like to work.

With the Matrix selected in the rack, and its associated sequencer track selected in the sequencer, select Edit > Copy Pattern to Track. This renders down the currently selected pattern to the sequencer. To copy another pattern, move the playhead, select the new pattern from the Matrix and repeat. A pattern must have note and level values present to be copied, otherwise nothing will happen. Remember to also move the L and R locators, as this is where Reason will put the sequencer data.

Once the data is in the main sequencer you can either drag and drop it to the sequencer track of another instrument to make it play back through that instrument, or re-assign the Matrix sequencer track to play back another module. The first option is probably easiest.

With the Matrix selected in the sequencer, play back the project whilst recording. Change the patterns in realtime as the track plays by pressing the pattern select buttons on the Matrix. Reason records these changes. Now when you play back, the matrix will swap patterns as you did when recording. The changes can be viewed and edited using the Pattern lane. The Matrix also gains a green outline box to show that it has been automated.

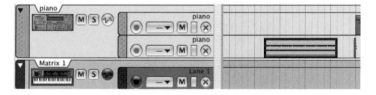

If you switch to Edit mode in the sequencer view, you will see that the Pattern lane for the Matrix has been activated. You will then see the patterns represented by blocks of colour on the timeline. Each new block corresponds to a pattern change. By using the dropdown menu on each clip to select one of the 32 patterns you can then take the pen tool and draw in instances of the pattern. This is basically the same as recording in realtime, but gives you more of a graphical view. Remember a Matrix can only play one pattern at once, so they can't overlap.

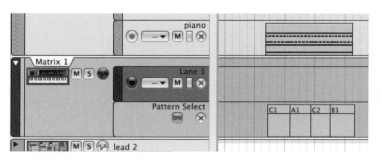

Recording

After a couple of hours spent playing with Reason you will probably have created your first tune. As is sometimes the case with software, there are often several ways of achieving the same things, and you can choose the one that suits you best. For example, it can be easier when making electronic or dance music to enter note information by hand using the pen tool, as you can create sequences and patterns that would be impossible to play by hand. By using a sustain pedal with your MIDI keyboard you can achieve more realistic piano and string sequences. In fact most traditionally keyboard-based patches benefit from the addition of a sustain pedal. For more experienced keyboard players it is fairly essential to have one. If you don't have one, the Edit mode lets you draw in sustain by hand, as well as a number of other parameters such as velocity, pitch and even breath control. This is covered in more detail in the preceding chapter.

If your MIDI keyboard has realtime controllers on it, Reason will read and remember any changes you make with them as it records. Reason 3,4 and 5 have the Remote system which allows you to control several devices from multiple keyboards or controllers at the same time, and record automation for them. In Reason 5 you can record note data on multiple sequencer tracks and lanes at once as well.

MIDI data exists independently of any instruments. Because of this, you can move or copy any notes in the sequencer to any track and have them played back by any instrument. This is useful for creating unusual passages

Figure 6.1
Edit mode allows you to draw sustain data in by hand, or edit it if it has already been recorded.

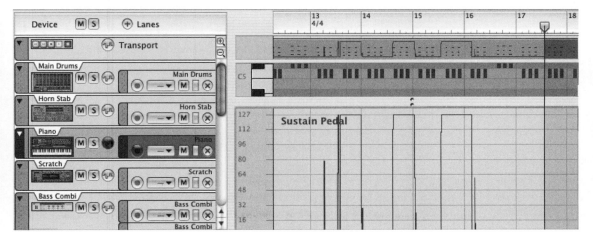

Figure 6.2 (right)
Reason supports the import of MIDI files. You can re-assign instruments to play the tracks.

Figure 6.3
Importing a standard MIDI file into an empty project will bring note data and sequencer tracks but will not load up any instruments.

– say, a piano part played back by a drum machine, and also for having several modules play exactly the same notes at the same time. At the other end of the scale, you can also import ready-made MIDI files created in other programs and simply reassign instruments to play them back.

MIDI information is basically a standard format, and so a MIDI file exported from one program should work in another. However, some programs will not support every

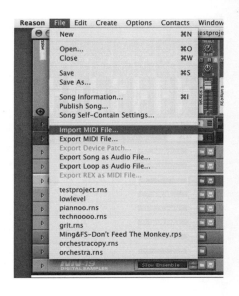

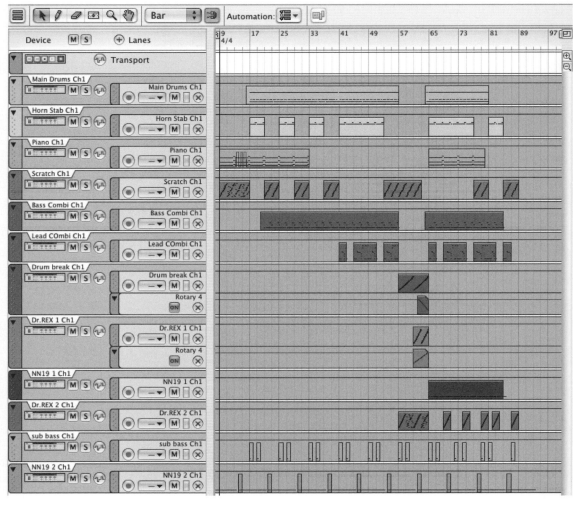

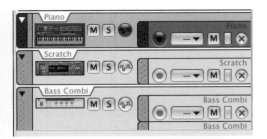

Figure 6.4
The red outline and darker track background mean MIDI input is being directed to that track.

parameter in the exported files. For instance, when exporting MIDI from Cubase SX to Reason, certain parts like VST instrument automation will not be translated, as there are no VST instruments in Reason.

MIDI files tend to contain note data but not Reason specific instrument data. If you import a MIDI file into Reason it will bring note data into the sequencer, as well as controller data like pitch bend, volume and mod wheel, but will not automatically load up the relevant modules and patches. If you are sharing files with other Reason users, use Reason song files rather than Standard MIDI files unless you specifically only need note or controller data to be sent.

As you create instruments in the rack, they appear as a list in the sequencer. The track which has its icon outlined in red is the one that will receive MIDI from the master keyboard. When you play MIDI in to it, it should show a green light to indicate input. Other keyboards can be assigned to other modules, as described below.

If you are playing loop-based rather than freeform music, setting the left and right markers and activating the loop button will cause Reason to cycle continuously between the two points. In Reason 3 There are two record modes – replace and overdub. In replace mode, Reason will get to the end of a cycle, start the loop again and delete the existing notes as it goes over them. Overdub adds to the loop as it goes round again, keeping and playing back the original notes as you go over them. This is handy for building complex loops, and is the mode most commonly used in practice. In Reason 4 and 5, you can use the New Dub and New Alt buttons to add extra note lanes to a sequencer track while recording, in order to overdub further notes or have a fresh take, muting the previous one. It's a better method than before because it lets you keep different takes or parts of a pattern on separate note lanes for easier editing. Clips can now be muted so you can bring parts of a loop in or out easily.

Figure 6.5
Lane-based record modes.

Figure 6.6
Recording to a click track is usually essential if you have no other rhythmic parts for reference.

Recording to a click track – at least until you have recorded a drum or rhythmic part for reference – will make your life much easier. Even if you are just improvising with a piano sound, if you capture a moment of genius it's much easier to then build the part into a song if it's been recorded in time

Figure 6.7
It's easier to see the effects of quantizing notes in Edit view.

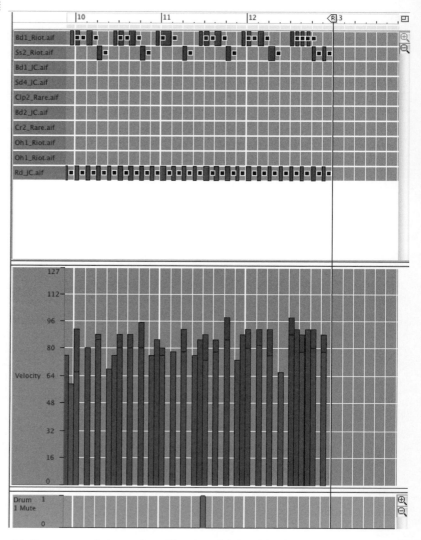

Figure 6.8
Use the Quantize Amount control in Reason 3 to stay in time but retain a natural feel to the music.

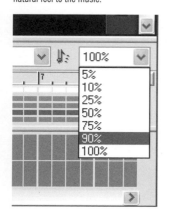

with the tempo of the project. Use the click level knob under the click on/off button to alter the volume of the click. The click track plays a high note, then three lower ones. The high note signifies the first beat of the bar. There's a pre-count button which gives you a count in - great if you have to get from the computer to the keyboard and need a guide to start playing.

Quantizing in Reason 3

Even experienced musicians can find it difficult to play precisely in time with a mechanical click track for the duration of several bars. After you have recorded notes in, some of them may be slightly (or wildly) out of sync with the click. As MIDI information is just a set of instructions, it can be made to behave how you want. In this case, you want to pull the notes into alignment with the grid. This process is called quantizing. It's often easier to see the results of quantizing by switching to the Edit view, where the notes can be seen much more

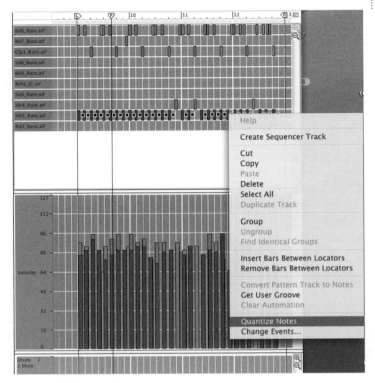

Figure 6.9
In Reason 3, Quantize different notes
using different values. In this example,
just the hi-hats within a drum pattern.

> **Tip**
>
> If you quantize a group of notes in Reason 3 it will change colour to show that it is different to the others around it. If a group has already been quantized and you try to quantize it again using the same settings, nothing will happen.

> **Tip**
>
> If you need to get really precise with notes, enter Edit mode and zoom in on the notes you want to edit. Switching to 1/64 quantize lets you snap notes marginally one way or the other. Turning off Snap to Grid gives you the freedom to move notes or groups of notes without Reason trying to pull them into time at all.

> **Tip**
>
> If you have a 'hit' in a song – say, a sample that needs to be triggered right at the beginning of a bar, quantize it using the Bar setting, and it will be snapped to the right place.

clearly. By selecting a quantize value (1/16 is often a safe bet) with your notes selected and pressing the quantize button, Reason will snap the notes to the nearest grid positions, bringing them into time. For more complex passages, more unusual quantize values are available.

A problem with quantizing is that it can make music, especially instruments like pianos, sound mechanical and a little too perfect. Luckily Reason has a Quantize Amount control, which lets you set just how strictly the notes are made to conform. Using a value of around 50 per cent balances out accuracy with a natural feel. There is also a button called Quantize Notes During Recording which if activated will snap notes to the grid as they are recorded. This can be useful for deliberately rhythmic parts like drums or synths, but can sound too regimented for other types of instrument. Remember you can always quantize after recording.

You can quantize individual notes or types of notes within a track. For example, say you have a ReDrum part that you've just played in by hand. You may want to quantize the hi-hats to a strict 1/16 setting, but the bass and snare to something a bit more fluid to maintain a funky feel. To do this, enter Edit mode and view the Drum Lane (which should be visible by default). You can see the drum part arranged in a grid. Draw around the hi-hats to select them and then set the quantize value to 1/16 and press the quantize button. The hi-hats are snapped, but the other parts of the beat are not. Then you can draw around the other parts by track or as a group, and quantize them as you want, or not at all. Snapping to lower values may actually reduce the number of notes you hear by regimenting them to stick to a certain subdivision of beats. For example, quantizing to 1/2 will snap notes to every other beat.

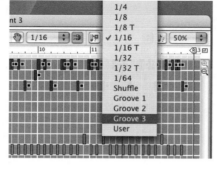

The Shuffle and Groove quantize settings apply snapping with a preset
amount of swing in it. These can be useful for funky, shuffling beats which are
still in time but less mechanical. Experimenting with them can produce interesting results.

You are not limited to preset quantize amounts. If you have played a
sequence with a unique feel to it, or you have a REX file with a particular timing, and want to make other notes snap to that same timing, you can use the
User Groove feature. Select the notes you want to 'extract' the groove from
and select Edit > Get User Groove. In the Quantize Type menu, the User
option is now available. Selecting different notes and quantizing them using
the User setting will copy the feel of the original to the new notes. You can
only store one User Groove at once, and it is not stored with the song file.

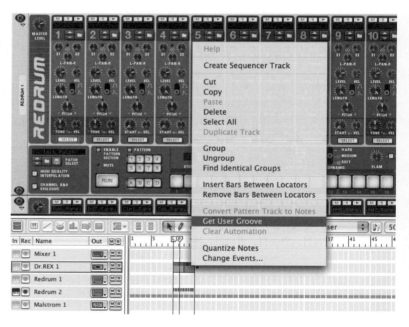

Change Events

There are some easier ways to edit certain parameters than just using the
tools. In Arrange or Edit mode, by selecting notes on one or more tracks and
selecting Edit > Change Events you can access some common editing functions. Transpose will shift the selected notes up or down by the desired num-

ber of semitones. This is very useful for creating variations in a song. For example, if you have created a great section of music and then want it to switch from playing in C to E to create a middle eight, or a natural progression, just copy and paste the notes, select the new groups and transpose. Instantly, the whole section of the track is playing in a different key.

Remember that transposing essentially shifts notes on a grid. This is fine as long as the keys all have notes assigned to them. If you transpose a REX file or a ReDrum pattern in this way, you won't change the pitch of the notes but rather the order in which they are played back. On the upside, this can be used to create some drum variations that you would never otherwise have thought of. Transposing REX drum loops in this way causes them to start on beats other than the first, which is often better than the original loop, or at the very least, great for pattern variations. To properly transpose a REX loop in the traditional sense, use the transpose knob on the front of the Dr.Rex player.

In the same way as Transpose, Velocity lets you alter velocity values for single or multiple notes. The Add field lets you enter a fixed value from 0 to 127, and the scale field lets you change velocities by a percentage. If you use the Add and Scale fields together you can change the dynamics of notes. For

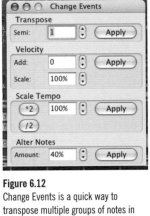

Figure 6.12
Change Events is a quick way to transpose multiple groups of notes in Reason 3.

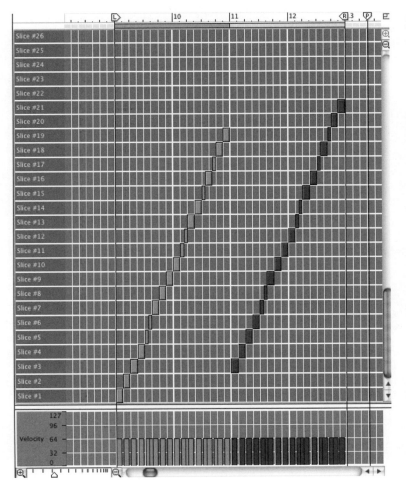

Figure 6.13
Transposing a REX lop from the Change Events menu will actually shift the order in which the notes play back

Info

If you transpose REX loops in this way you may find that there is some empty space at the end of the loop. Use Edit mode to copy and paste, or the pen tool to draw in some notes to fill out the loop.

Info

You can stop and start your song while the Change Events window is open, letting you instantly hear the results of your changes.

Info

If you choose Edit > Select All and use the Change Events controls, you can affect the entire track. Remember that you may not want to alter rhythm tracks in the same way as instrument tracks.

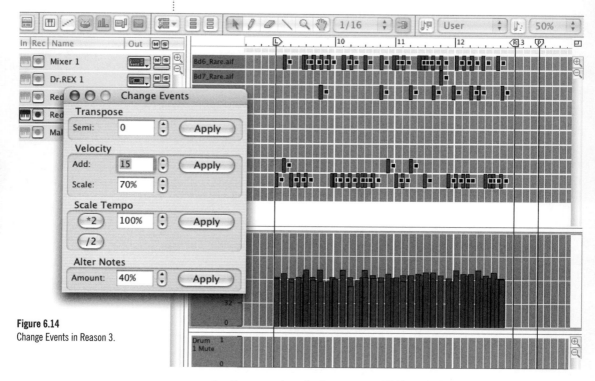

Figure 6.14
Change Events in Reason 3.

example, if you scale velocity to, say, 70% and also add an amount greater than ten or so, you can effectively compress the notes, in the sense that you will reduce the difference between the velocity values without lowering the average velocity (Figure 6.14).

Tip

Alter Notes is great to use with REX loops, as it creates some variations without changing important properties like the feel of the loop.

The Scale Tempo control makes notes play back faster or slower. Use the x2 and /2 controls to quickly half or double the speed, or enter a value in the box. The Alter Notes control is a great way of adding variations to loops or parts. It randomizes the pitch, length and velocity of notes. The higher the value you enter, the greater the variation. It does however stay within the note range of the existing notes, so in effect it is shuffling what's already there around rather than placing notes at completely random pitches and velocities (Figure 6.15).

Figure 6.15

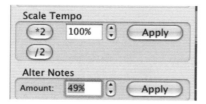

Locking Surfaces

A new feature in Reason 3 was the ability to assign specific controllers to individual devices in the rack and it is also present in Reason 4 and 5. This is useful for playing live, but also for recording. There are many situations in which you might want to have more than one device recorded at the same time. Imagine for example that you have programmed a drumbeat over four or five minutes. You could then set up multiple keyboards, locked to devices and several people could use the system at the same time, and the results of controlling other modules in the rack recorded as you went along. Or if it was just you, set up a controller locked to the mixer and another as a master keyboard. Now you can have control over levels, mute and solo in the mixer, as well as being able to play any instrument by directing MIDI to it in the sequencer.

Quantizing in Reason 4 and 5

Reason 4 and 5 take a different approach to quantizing than previous versions of the program. Some of the same techniques apply, but many of the tools have been moved or modified. Notes are now automatically created and contained within clips when you record, rather than you having to group them manually. You can activate the Quantize During Record button from the transport. However many MIDI functions have now moved to the new Tool window, and in its Tools tab you will find the quantize functions. With one or more clips selected, or notes within a clip when in Edit mode, you can choose the quantize value and amount from this window, and there's a new Random setting to introduce random variations into the pattern for a more natural feel. Many of the functions from the old Change Events window are now collected in the other tabs here, including note length, tempo adjustments, velocity and transpose, all of which affect the clips or notes you have selected.

You can also use the snap setting to govern the way clips will behave when being moved, shortened or lengthened.

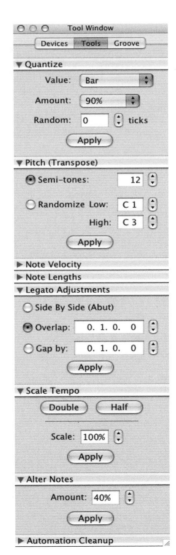

Figure 6.16 (a)
The MIDI functions in the Tool Window.

Reason 4 and 5 have an entirely new system for groove quantizing parts, called the ReGroove Mixer. See the ReGroove chapter for a detailed breakdown of this, but in essence it provides an alternative to the standard quantizing that Reason has had up until now. By activating the ReGroove mixer, making settings in its slots and then routing sequencer tracks through those slots, you can quantize tracks on the fly – i.e. non-destructively – and get complete control over the way they feel. Much more flexible than regular quantizing, it lets you tweak all aspects of shuffle, slide and groove, from a slight alteration to a huge change. If you press the Pre Align button for a ReGroove slot, its notes will be auto-snapped to a 1/16 grid in realtime prior to passing through the ReGroove Mixer, so you don't even have to worry about that.

Figure 6.16 (b)
The ReGroove Mixer quantizing parts in real time.

Settings for the ReGroove channels can be made on the channel itself or in greater depth in the Groove tab on the Tool window.

Figure 6.16 (c)

Surface Locking

If you have specified a master keyboard, it cannot be locked to a device. You can however choose to Use No Master Keyboard in the preferences. If you do this, you will be able to lock it to a device and tweak the controls, but not play it using the keys. Information about locked devices is saved with your song file.

Figure 6.17 (a)
Choose whether or not to use a master MIDI keyboard.

A number of control surfaces can be locked to the same device, but each can only be locked to one device at a time. If the Reason module has more controls than your controller, say, the mixer for example, you can assign more than one controller to it and customise the setup so that between the controllers, all the parameters on the mixer can be used in realtime.

Access surface locking controls either by selecting Options > Surface Locking, or by control + clicking (Mac) or right-clicking (PC) on a device and selecting the Lock to option. Remember that if you only have one keyboard and have specified it to be the master, this option will not appear in the contextual menu. You can unlock a device in the same way as locking it.

Figure 6.17 (b)

Remote Override

A feature of this realtime control system is the ability to customise remote control maps. This is especially useful if you don't have a fully-featured USB controller, but rather a more generic MIDI keyboard with few or no realtime control knobs or sliders. Here are some things to know about this mode.

Access it either by selecting Options > Remote Override Edit Mode or control + click (Mac) or right click (PC) on a parameter and selecting Edit Remote Override Mapping.

Figure 6.18
Remote Override Edit mode, for assigning controllers.

Figure 6.19
A module displaying which of its parameters can be controlled in realtime.

Accessed from the Options menu, modules are greyed out and the one you select gets highlighted. Parameters that can be controlled are shown using blue arrows. Double-click a parameter to activate MIDI learn. Move the control or note you wish to map and a tooltip appears to tell you it's been successfully assigned.

Accessed via the contextual menu, you get a more conventional MIDI learn window, from where you can assign controls in the more traditional way. On most modules, patch select buttons can be controlled, meaning a key press can cycle between patches.

If you use a key on the keyboard to assign to a parameter, it will change values between zero and 100 per cent – like an on/off button. So for example, a fader on the mixer can be set to zero or full using a key press. As long as you remember what triggers what, you could set up a basic keyboard just to control channels on/off in the mixer. Using masking tape on the keys with simple instructions is a good way to set up a controller in this way.

You can copy and paste Remote Overrides between devices of the same type. In Remote Override Edit mode you can choose a device with mappings and use the Edit menu to copy and paste the mappings to another device – e.g from ReDrum to ReDrum, or Dr.Rex to Dr.Rex. If pasting to the same project you are

Tip

In the Preferences > Keyboards section, choose Standard or Separated Master Keyboard input. The first always directs the master keyboard to the selected track. The second lets you select tracks independently of the master keyboard.

Info

You cannot map the same key or controller to more than one parameter.

Tip

Remove remote overrides in the same way as you assign them, by control or right clicking.

Figure 6.20
The contextual menu brings up a MIDI
learn window.

Tip

Pressing the escape key will
instantly jump you out of
Remote Override Edit mode.

prompted to choose which of the two you want to have the mappings, as the
same keys can't be mapped to more than one device. If you're pasting to a different project, there's no problem.

Figure 6.21
Remote control maps can be pasted
between devices within a project, but if
they conflict you have to choose one or
the other.

Tip

In Remote Override Edit Mode you
can clear all mappings for a
device in a single go by selecting it
and choosing Clear from the Edit
menu.

If you select Options > Additional Remote Overrides, you can assign some
system-specific commands to controllers or keys. Various parameters like undo
/ redo, select next / previous track, go to locators and so on can be assigned.
This is particularly useful in a live or live recording situation, as it won't break
your flow or cause you to have to come back to the mouse and the keyboard
to perform these tasks.

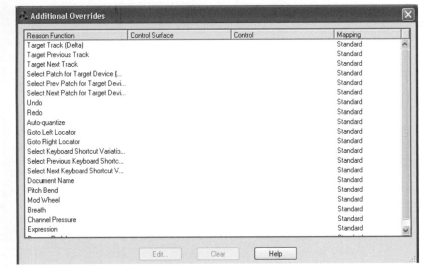

Figure 6.22
Additional Remote Overrides let you
perform some system tasks from a MIDI
controller.

Tip

Standard Remote mapping for
supported control surfaces is
always available in Reason. If you
create a custom setup for your
unsupported kit, it's best to save it
as a template containing the
devices and mappings but no
sequencer data so the controls will
be available every time you open
it. Remember to always re-save it
as a different filename.

Keyboard Control

This function is a bit like Remote, only it works using the computer's keyboard, and can only be used to toggle things on or off, or values between zero and 100 per cent. It involves no MIDI data, just commands. It's sort of an extension of Reason's other key commands for saving, undoing and that sort of thing. To switch it on, choose Options > Enable keyboard Control. To assign keys, either enter Keyboard Control Edit Mode from the same menu, or right-click (PC) or control-click (Mac) on a parameter. Assigning commands is then done in the same way as with Remote, only the arrows are yellow. There is no crossover between Remote and Keyboard control, as one uses MIDI and the other does not. It works using something like the MIDI learn function, only with key presses.

Figure 6.23
Keyboard Control mode lets you assign certain commands to your computer keyboard.

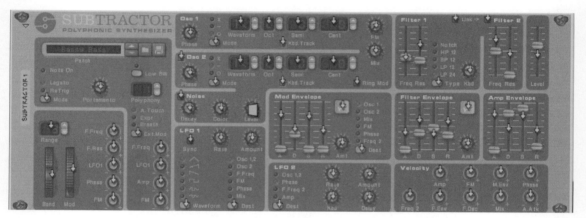

There are several uses for this:

* Setting up the numeric keys 1 to 0 to solo mixer channels.
* Assigning a row of keys to mute faders on the mixer.
* Setting up the numeric keypad to switch between patterns on a Matrix or a ReDrum.
* Assigning a key command to switch the mod wheel on a sampler from zero to full.
* Bypassing an effect with a key press

Basically, any parameter that comes up with a yellow arrow in Keyboard Control Edit mode can be assigned a key command. This is yet another way for you to customise Reason.

Loading your own samples

The NN-19 and NN-XT samplers both have two file load buttons. The first is to select patches designed for the module, but the second will load raw .WAV or AIFF audio files which can be played from the MIDI keyboard. Because they are individual samples they will get higher and faster as you go up the keyboard, and lower and slower as you go down. Sometimes this is desirable, sometimes not, but it does mean that you can use your own loops. In a typ-

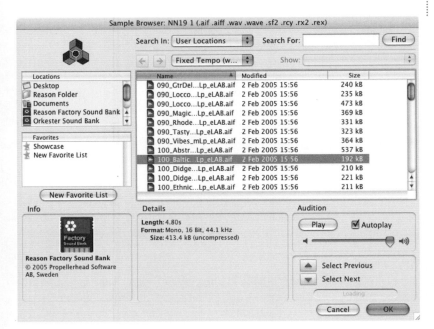

Figure 6.24
The samplers and drum machine in Reason are able to load any audio file you have recorded in another program.

ical example you might record a guitar riff or a vocal into a wave editing package like Sound Forge or Peak then export it as an audio file. By loading this into one of Reason's samplers you can use it in your song. The sound doesn't go into the sequencer, rather a MIDI note is recorded to trigger the sample, just like with real hardware samplers. The NN-XT and ReDrum are able to load samples in more advanced ways. See their specific chapters for more on this.

Sampling

What is sampling?

Those with memories stretching back a decade or two will remember that when people used to say something was a 'sampler', it meant that it could record and play back digital audio in some way. As software has gradually taken over the world of sampling, many of the new devices commonly referred to as samplers have in fact been sample playback modules. To sample your audio you had to record it elsewhere, either in hardware, in a DAW or in a wave editor. This applied to a certain extent to Reason, where many people called the the NN-19 and NN-XT samplers when in fact they are sample players, able to load and manipulate pre-recorded audio and even organise collections of samples into instruments, but not record.

This has been the way things were done in Reason for so long that people just sort of got used to it but in truth, as a process it was more fiddly than many people would have liked. Reason 5 introduces live sampling wherever you see the wave icon. Any module that can load an audio sample can now also record samples from any connected audio source. So with your interface set up, you can sample in from a mic, turntables, a CD player, guitar, bass or anything else you can think of. The clever part is that the sampling is total-

Figure 6.25
Route any available audio input to the
Sampling Inputs by spinning the rack
around and heading to the top.

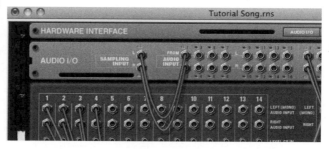

ly integrated into the software. You don't have to sample into a track or into
a pool of audio, you just record directly into any compatible module and
Reason does the rest. Samples are stored inside the project file, so there's
no need to worry about where they live and when you duplicate or copy a
project file, all the recorded samples will be carried across to the new file.

Why sample?

Sampling has become something of a lost art for many musicians and producers, thanks largely to the advent of professionaly produced sample collections and virtual instruments. Indeed for some people, these are an ideal
way to quickly build backing tracks or embellish your own productions. The
process of self-sampling though is one that can yield all kinds of unexpectedly great results and has the added benefit of making your tracks sound
more unique. After all if you are using a popular sample collection to build
your tracks the chances are that others will be doing the same with the same
loops. This even applies to Reason's Sound Bank, loops from which pop up
regularly on TV soundtracks and adverts. If however you make your own samples, nobody else will have access to those sounds and you are able to claim
a much greater stake in having created something original. Many people
have a signature sound, a collection of guitar pedals or a way of recording
vocals through an old megaphone that they feel gives their music a certain
sound and feel. Capturing this in Reason can help to really stamp your sound
on your projects.

The key to all this and the reason that this new tool is likely to kick start
a resurgence of interest in sampling your own material is that it's just so
incredibly easy to do. Anyone who started life sampling in hardware may
remember how tedious it could be, setting start and end points, getting it
wrong and setting up keygroups, working with a few small buttons and a tiny
screen. It was something you really had to learn about before you got any
good at it. The way it is implemented in Reason couldn't be much more different. Click on a sampling button on any compatible module and a sampling
window appears. With your audio input correctly set up in the Preferences
and in the Sampling Input module at the top of the rack, hit the Record button and whatever you play or sing in to Reason is captured.

Info

You may have a mixing desk or
audio interface with multiple
audio channels available. If you
wanted to have several sources
connected at once – say a mic,
guitar and CD player, you could
connect these physically, make a
note of their input channel
numbers and then switch the
audio input channel on Reason's
Audio I/O module to make that
channel the sampling input.

Figure 6.26
Click the Sampling button wherever you
see it to sample straight into that
module.

Tip

In the sample record window,
capturing starts as soon as you
hit the sampling icon. To start
again without exiting the window,
hit the 'return to start' icon on the
sampling window.

Sample editing

After recording your sample, you can edit it in a number of ways using the
mini floating sample window found in Reason 5. This lets you perform a number of tasks including normalizing, looping and cropping the sample and
there's a handy option to automatically set the loop points around the beginning and end of the waveform.

Once the sample is in the module it can be controlled and edited using
the tools that have always been available on the ReDrum, NN-19 and NN-XT
as well as now the NN-Nano sampler inside the Kong Drum Designer. These
let you alter pitch and length, play with filters and ADSR controls and more
advanced things like creating whole sampled instruments combining velocity
switching, layers and keyboard zoning in the case of NN-XT.

Sampling your own instruments note by note is something that had previously required a dedicated software or hardware sampler but now, although
it is at the more advanced end of what you might want to do in Reason, it is
perfectly possible, especially with the NN-XT.

Understanding sampling in Reason 5

1 For the first time, Reason can accept audio input for the purposes of
   recording. You can configure this in the Audio Preferences section. In the
   rack, go to the Sampling Input module at the top and check that the
   audio is routed in correctly. Press tab to spin the rack round and
   manually patch cables if necessary.
2 The Big Meter and audio input meters should show you if your audio is
   too loud or too quiet, Aim to have it around 0dB or +4dB at its loudest.
   Create a module that can sample – say, an NN-19. Click on the Start
   Sampling button located to the right of the sample load button.
3 Sampling will start immediately, so play or say something in, through a
   microphone or using a guitar or other direct source. Don't worry about
   starting immediately, just start when you are ready. Once you have
   finished, click on the Edit button to open the floating sample editor
   window.
4 In the editor window you can select some or all of the sample and choose
   to normalize it, reverse it, fade it in or out or crop it. If you select a
   section you can press Set Sample Start/End to select that section.
   Alternatively manually drag the two markers or hit Snap to Transients.

5   As you are doing this, you can audition the sample using the Play button and hear it in isloation by choosing Solo. You can also name it here and set up the sample as a loop with different loop modes, plus the option to crossfade the loop to prevent any clicks as it starts playing over again.

6   The sample is now playable from the NN-19. If you open the Tool window and go to the new sample tab you will see that all samples in a project can be viewed, edited, deleted, duplicated or exported out of Reason. Clicking Edit will reopen the floating editor window.

Building a beatbox kit in ReDrum

1   Create a ReDrum. You may want to start with a patch and replace various samples but here, why not try choosing Edit > Initialize Patch to wipe the module clear. With your audio I/O set up as described above, hit the wave icon on channel 1 and record a sample in.

2   Use the Edit window to trim your sample down, since in most drum kits or beatboxes the sounds will need to be quite short. You can use longer samples but these will of course play themselves out when triggered, unless you play with the Length setting on the respective ReDrum channel.

3   Repeat with as many channels as you need, recording a new sound into each one. Feel free to use any sound you can make, to create unusual kits. It's well worth naming samples clearly as you do this, as otherwise you can end up with a ton of samples with no helpful names.

4   With your kit recorded, try programming a beat, either using the key editor in the sequencer or using the onboard pattern sequencer. If your samples sound a little 'late' when sequenced you may need to reopen the sample editor and set the start point a little later. Experiment until each sample comes in exactly on time.

5   Take advantage of ReDrum's separate channel outputs by processing some hits individually. Try placing the device inside a Combinator by selecting Edit > Combine, then using a variety of effects and line mixers to process say the snare and one other channel through some delay or reverb, leaving the other channels dry.

6   Using the controls on the ReDrum's channels you can also do some extensive tweaking, altering various parameters for each sound. These include level, length, pitch, pan and tone. Use these to further tweak and tune your kit until it sounds just right. Consider saving the Combi patch for future use.

The sample editor

The sample edit window is really useful, providing the tools you need to work with your recorded audio. For a start it guesses with some accuracy where the start of the sample is based on the transients, and sets the start point there. There's also an option to automatically set the start and end points.

Some features of the sample edit window

- A zoom function to help you work on small areas in more detail
- An option to set a crossfade loop, great for ironing out small glitches at the point a loop crosses over.

Tip

Immediately after finishing recording a sample, hit the Edit button to be taken to the sample editor. To edit it later, go to the Tool window's Song Samples section and locate it under the Self-Contained Samples section. Double click a sample to open it in the editor.

Tip

In the Sample Editor window you can name a sample, which makes it much easier to keep track of.

- Undo and redo functions in cas you change your mind while editing
- Important processing functions including crop, normalize, reverse and fade in and out.
- Set the loop mode, either one shot, loop forward or loop forward and backwards.
- Set the volume of a sample independently of the track or module it is on
- Set the root key or a sample, good for building multisampled instruments.

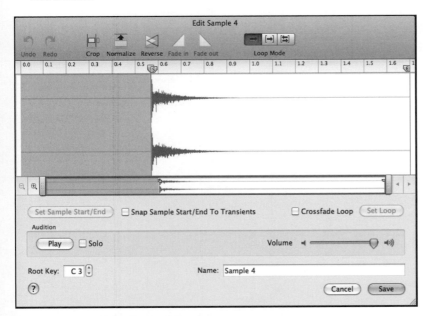

Figure 6.27
The sample edit window lets you work with audio you have sampled.

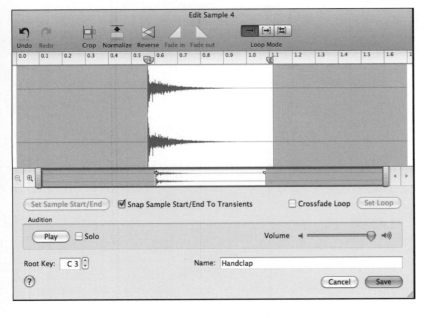

Figure 6.28
Give samples unique names and set start and end points automatically or manually.

Figure 6.29
Select some or all of a sample's waveform and perform processing functions on it like normalize or reverse.

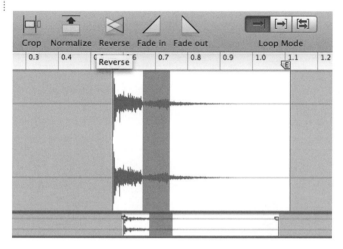

Uses for live sampling

In more everyday situations there are tons of practical uses for quick and easy sampling, and the fact that it is integrated directly into the rack means you are much more likely to make it a part of your workflow. Perhaps the most obvious example might be creating your own beatbox kit or drum kit in a ReDrum by sampling different material onto each of its channels. Or you may have a great ReDrum patch but want to add a couple of different sounds, say some vocal stabs. Locate a channel that's not in use and replace the sound in that channel with a sample of your own. If you are working with more cut-up music like hip hop, you could keep it old school with the NN-19, recording a single sample into it and triggering it from your keyboard. Or for something more complex, use the NN-XT to record multiple samples and then experiment with layering them up, creating velocity switches or key zones.

By using the Combinator you could even combine several of these modules together to build really huge instruments consisting of your own sampled material. Export them and share them online, even sell them in cases where all the content is your own. The possibilities are endless, and it's not just great for music that is traditionally sample-based either. The ability to drop your own sounds straight into a project will come in handy for everything from trance to rock. Whether you use your own samples as the basis of entire tracks or to add your own unique character and signature to tracks that use other samples and instrument patches, you will be glad that you discovered just how easy it is to sample in Reason and also where the two programs are installed on the same system, in Record.

Figure 6.30
Managing samples in a project in the Tool window.

Automation

Automation used to be a feature only of high-end studio hardware. Happily, it's now available to a much wider audience including Reason users. The concept is simple – record the movement of controls as you move them. Then when you play back, the controls move by themselves. Software affords us huge possibilities on this front, as it tends to be more flexible than hardware.

One of the most common types of automation is mixer automation. You

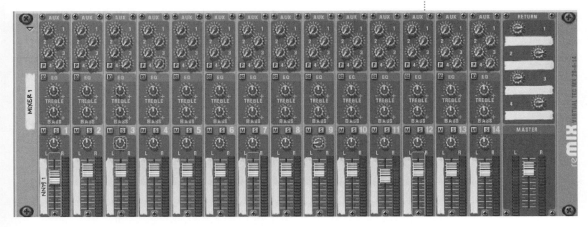

Figure 6.31
An automated mixer, displaying green boxes around controls that have been recorded.

can use this to make faders, pan and EQ controls, for example, move by themselves. Automating a mix makes creating interesting tracks much easier. For instance, you may have a piano line that plays loud in the chorus but quietly during the verse. Rather than duplicating parts onto different tracks, just automate the fader at the right point so that the volume increases and decreases by itself. The same principle applies to automating anything (Figure 6.31).

Before you record automation it's a good idea to set a controller to the value it's supposed to have when it's not being automated. This is because Reason takes this to be its 'static' value and as soon as you start recording, will insert this value throughout the song for that parameter. You can see this graphically if you view the automation subtrack lane. To prevent controls from jumping around unexpectedly, this is a good move. For example, to create a fade out, make sure the fader is at its normal value before you start to automate the fade out. Reason will then know that at every point previous to the start of the fade, the fader should be at that original value.

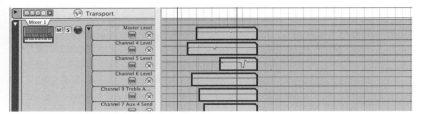

Figure 6.32
Reason inserts values as soon as you start automating a control .

If a device is to be automated, it must have a track in the sequencer. Instruments should automatically have one, but mixers and effects will not. Select the mixer and choose Create > Sequencer Track, then assign the mixer to it using the icon box in the sequencer track view. Alternatively, right-click (PC) or control-click (Mac) on the mixer and select Create > Sequencer Track for Mixer. All devices can be assigned sequencer tracks in this way, except devices with no realtime controls such as the two Spider devices, the Hardware Interface and the ReBirth input machine.

Automation is recorded by pressing play and record, and using the controls you want to automate. In Reason 2.5 the track that is to be automated

Info

Before you can automate any device it must have a sequencer track. This includes the mixer and effect devices.

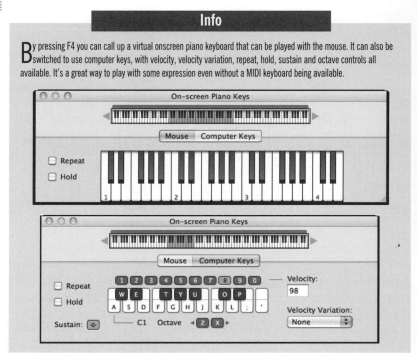

Info

By pressing F4 you can call up a virtual onscreen piano keyboard that can be played with the mouse. It can also be switched to use computer keys, with velocity, velocity variation, repeat, hold, sustain and octave controls all available. It's a great way to play with some expression even without a MIDI keyboard being available.

must have the MIDI icon next to it in the sequencer. In Reason 3 and higher, automation can be recorded on multiple tracks at once. Simply press the red record button for every track you want to automate. This is ideal if you take advantage of the multiple controller support and have several people

Tip

As well as automating in realtime using the mouse, you can enter Edit mode, select any available parameter from the Controllers menu, and draw automation in with the pen or line tools.

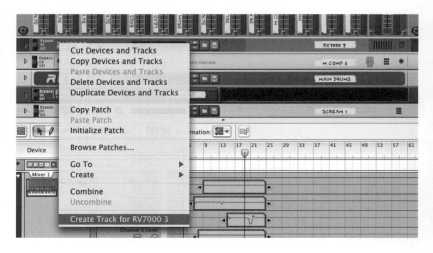

Figure 6.33
Create a sequencer track if you want to automate non-instrument devices.

playing the system at once. All their controller movements will be recorded. In Reason 5, you can record notes as well as automation on multiple sequencer tracks.

If you have automated a parameter and want to redo or change it, you can use the tools in Edit mode. Alternatively, go back over the same section whilst recording and 'grab' the controller at any point. Reason will overwrite the automation from the point you start to change it. The Automation Override on the Transport Panel will light up to signify that you have done this (Figure 6.29).

You can still 'grab' a controller at any point, even if it has been automated, to temporarily regain control of it. Imagine you have programmed a fade but decide on the spur of the moment to drop the channel straight out or straight in. You don't have to be recording, and if you move that controller, its automation will be disabled for as long as Reason plays back. As soon as you stop and start playback, automation is re-enabled.

With a bit of clever automation you can create much more professional sounding tracks, more interesting synth sounds and effects. If you control-click or right-click on a parameter you can select Edit Automation, which will transfer the sequencer view straight to the automation subtrack for that parameter. If you alt-click (Mac) or control-click (PC) on a parameter, Reason will jump straight to its automation subtrack.

Figure 6.34
Recording automation on several tracks at once in Reason.

Automation in Reason 4 and 5

In Reason 4 the automation system had an overhaul and is now vector based, meaning it works using a series of points and linear segments. This makes it much more accurate to work with compared to the free flowing values from previous versions. You no longer have to go into Edit mode to view and edit automation data, it can be done from the Arrage view as well. For any automatable parameter – which is practically any parameter in Reason – if you move it while recording, its sequencer track will gain a new lane displaying that parameter's automation. If you want to draw data in, use the pen tool to draw a clip, then double click it to expand that lane while still in Arrange view. There, you can draw, pick up, drag and delete vector points to control automation. By double clicking on clips you can expand them and make them editable, and clips can be shortened or lengthened easily.

Figure 6.35
Automation Override engaged in Reason 5.

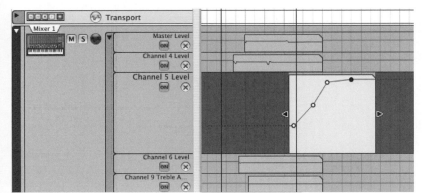

Figure 6.36
Editing automation points from Arrange view.

When you select a point, its value appears in the Value box. To manually set the point to a specific value, choose it and then type a new value into the box. This way you can get very precise control over your automation. The static value – the value present before automation starts – is displayed as a blue line.

Figure 6.37
Making precise automation settings.

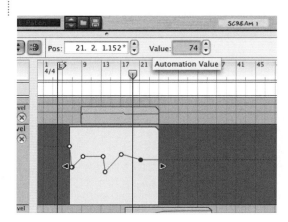

If you do go into Edit mode you can get a much clearer view of the automation lanes and zoom in and out using the zoom controls. Double click on a clip to make its points editable. You also get a level display showing you the static value.

Automation data can be recorded either as performance controller or track parameter data. You control this setting using the 'Automation as Perf Ctrl' button on the transport. Performance controller data like pitch bend or mod wheel is recorded as part of a note clip. Track parameter data is recorded on fresh note lanes, in addition to the original note lane. If you wish you can force the recording of track parameters into the note clip by pressing the button. This makes it easier to move and copy all the data as one. The trade-off is it becomes harder to view the different automated parameters separately. You also won't be able to mute the separate automation lanes or move them independently as they will exist as performance controllers like sustain, pitch bend and so on.

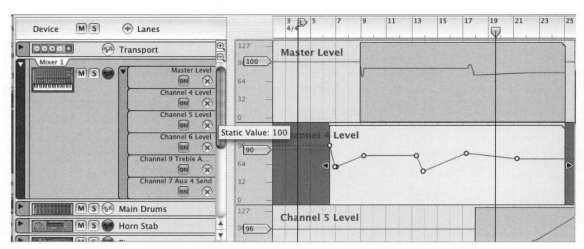

Figure 6.38
Viewing automation in Edit mode.

Editing automation using vector points is much quicker and easier than previously and can be performed while playing back. When editing automation, you can multiple select vector points by dragging a box around them. Frequently when you are drawing points or curves there will be too many but

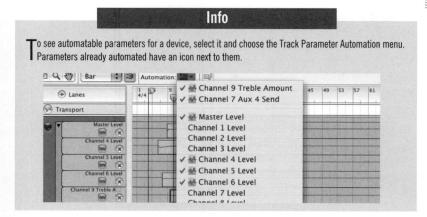

Info

To see automatable parameters for a device, select it and choose the Track Parameter Automation menu. Parameters already automated have an icon next to them.

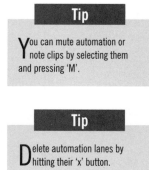

Tip

You can mute automation or note clips by selecting them and pressing 'M'.

Tip

Delete automation lanes by hitting their 'x' button.

as soon as you release the mouse they will be reduced to just a few necessary to make the transition. This is called Automation Cleanup and is controlled globally from the Tools section of the Tool window or the General section of the preferences. Set low, Reason will leave many points. Set to maximum, it deletes all but the most essential. You can select groups of points and apply cleanup settings at any point using the Apply button on the Tool window, Automation Cleanup tab.

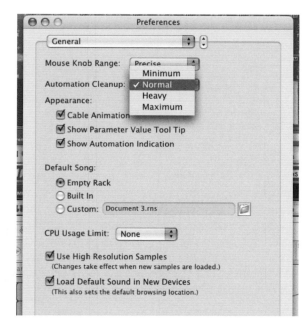

Figure 6.39
Automation Cleanup.

Automating tempo and time signature

Reason 4 and 5 can automate tempo and time signature, meaning that you can create much more varied and interesting tracks, as well as matching Reason projects to other material with varying tempo like live performances or films. It works very much like other automation, and is operated from the Transport track in the sequencer.

To automate tempo, simply draw in values with the pen tool. It can be helpful to manually enter exact values using the Value box. To go from one tempo to another, draw a start and end point with the pen tool. To quickly create a ramp, draw it with the pen tool. If there are errant points imbetween the start and end, draw round them and delete them. This will cause the line to go simply from the first to the last point in a ramp. Remember that Snap applies when inserting points.

Figure 6.40
Activating tempo automation.

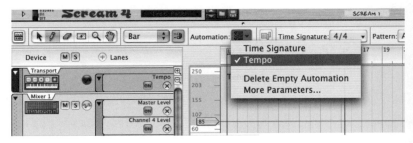

Figure 6.41
Before deleting errant automation points.

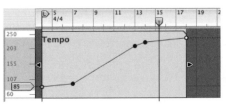

Figure 6.42
... and after.

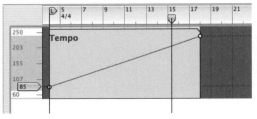

Tip

ou can alter the position of points by selecting them and entering precise values in the Position box.

Tip

Although Reason can deal with subdivisions of BPM like 80.322 BPM, you'll generally want to stick to round values like 80.

To automate Time Signature, the process is similar to pattern automation on a ReDrum or a Matrix. You can't transition between time signatures as you can with tempo – you're either at one or the other so Reason has to switch at an exact point. Activate time signature automation and use the pen tool to draw clips into the new automation lane. Each clip can represent a time signature change, and you choose the value by clicking on it – just like pattern automation. These have to run for as long as you want them to be active. As soon as the playhead reaches a point where a time signature automation clip ends, it will flip back to the default 4/4.

Figure 6.43
Time signature automation.

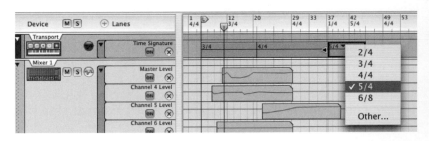

Automating tempo and time signature is a great way to add depth and interest to your tracks, and is very straightforward in Reason. Clips can be easily copied, pasted, dragged and tempo clips can be muted. All clips in the sequencer can be labelled to make them easier to identify at a glance.

Tip

Time signatures display in the ruler section of the sequencer.

Tip

When in ReWire mode, tempo and time signature information in Reason are ignored and only information from the host sequencer like Cubase will be read. However when you return to standalone mode, the data will affect Reason as normal.

The ReGroove Mixer

What it is

The original application of MIDI as a technology was for triggering sound sources like synths, drum machines and later, workstations. It allowed you to create a certain type of feel and style of playing that would shape electronic music for many years. The mechanical, robotic regularity of MIDI-triggered parts can be heard all over countless records from the turn of the 1980s onwards. It also makes possible the creation of parts that couldn't be played by hand, either because they are too fast or too complex, or because the creator of the music wasn't necessarily a skilled keyboard player. As MIDI has become an integral part of music technology, simply snapping or quantizing notes rigidly to a grid is no longer enough for many musicians. Now, people want to be able to infuse their MIDI tracks with that most indefinable of characteristics – a human feel. Reason has for a while had a groove extraction and quantize feature to address this need, and to an extent is was successful. The one drawback is that changes had to be applied to notes, so if you wanted to change them later you had to undo the changes or apply further modification to the notes. Wouldn't it be better to be able to treat timing a bit like audio is processed through effects? That is, in a form that is non-permanent and can be edited on the fly?

Figure 7.1
Show and hide the ReGroove Mixer.

Reason's ReGroove Mixer provides the answer to this conundrum. Resembling a stripped down audio mixer, and working on a similar basic principle, it lurks behind the Transport Panel, hidden and shown with a simple button. It has eight slots and four banks, for a total of 32 channels. Each channel contains controls to modify the quantize, shuffle and groove settings of the data which is routed through it. The revamped sequencer allows any note lane to be assigned to any of these 32 channels. Remember that although this sounds similar to effect routing, what is happening is that the notes are being processed, not the sound. ReGroove works independently of the devices in the rack.

The ReGroove Mixer shouldn't be confused with the audio mixers in Reason. It intercepts notes as they travel from the sequencer to the modules in the rack, thereby changing the eventual pattern that is played. It's only after the notes have been triggered that sound is generated – sound which is dealt with by audio mixers. It can be active whilst hidden to save you screen space, and even when it's hidden you can access all of the controls for each of its 32 slots using the Groove tab on the Tool window.

What it does

The Regroove Mixer acts as a realtime, non-destructive quantizer for notes in sequencer tracks. Normally, you have to quantize notes using specific settings on a sequencer track. With ReGroove, although you can still do that, you can also get much better control over the quantize and groove settings and have them applied on-the-fly, editable at any time and leaving your original notes unaffected. Think of it like passing audio through an effect unit, only now you're passing MIDI notes through a MIDI effect of sorts. The idea is that traditional forms of quantizing are both restrictive and clumsy, since they have only basic settings and also require you to "glue down" the changes to groups of notes. Whilst regular quantizing can tidy up a performance, the results are often too strict, too rigid and mechanical. You can get away with this in some forms of electronic music but it can strip the life out of others.

Features of the channel strip

Figure 7.2
A ReGroove channel strip.

- The on button activates or deactivates the slot. When set to On, any sequencer tracks routed through the slot will be processed. Switched off, the data passes through unchanged. Use this as a mute button or A/B function to hear the notes with and without groove processing.
- The Edit button opens the Tool window at the Groove tab, letting you make detailed settings about how the notes are processed. Clicking the Edit button for successive slots means the Tool Window will change the slot whose informationit displays.
- The Name field, when clicked, opens links to other patches in the current folder, and the file browser. The arrow buttons navigate up and down the list of patches in the folder, and the Folder button opens the file browser.
- The fader controls the amount of groove applied. The Slide control slides notes fractionally back or forwards in time, creating a rushed or a lazy feel. Shuffle adds a sixteenth note swing to the notes.
- The Pre-Align button forces notes to be quantized to a sixteenth note grid immediately before having groove applied so that the results are as expected. This is nondestructive and saves you manually quantizing notes in the sequencer first.
- The Global Shuffle button forces a ReGroove channel to use the global shuffle setting – handy for sync'ing with other devices using this setting, like the RPG-8, Matrix or ReDrum's sequencer.
- The Anchor Point setting on the left of the mixer tells Reason at which measure in a bar it should start applying the groove settings. Where a sequence starts somewhere other than the first measure, you can set here where the groove will start. If you insert a time signature change into a project, grooves will restart when they encounter it.

Figure 7.3
The ReGroove Mixer.

Routing notes to ReGroove channels

Each sequencer track is now able to accommodate a number of lanes, and each lane can be routed to a ReGroove channel. In the most basic example you would simply route the default lane 1 to a slot by clicking on its Select Groove menu and choosing a slot. You can route any number of sequencer lanes through a single ReGroove slot if you want them to share the same settings. Note that you can prevent a lane from being sent by unchecking its Enabled menu option. You can also make a groove permanent – that is, render it down to the MIDI notes – by selecting Commit to Groove. You may need to do this if for example you want to edit notes in their groove quantized form, without the realtime quantizing still taking place.

Be aware that if you use the Commit to Groove option, it renders down all note lanes with groove enabled for that sequencer track. To get around this, temporarily uncheck the Enabled option for any lanes on that track that you wish to leave untouched (i.e. with notes on the track physically unchanged), perform the Commit function which will affect any lanes still enabled, then switch Enabled back on for the lanes you had momentarily switched off.

Info

ReGroove presets are stored with a project. They can be saved as .grov files using the Save button on the Groove section of the Tool window.

Tip

Right click on a ReGroove channel to find the options to initialize it or copy its settings to the clipboard. You can then paste a setting to another channel.

Tip

The knobs and fader on a ReGroove channel can be mapped to a realtime MIDI controller just like controls on synths and audio mixers.

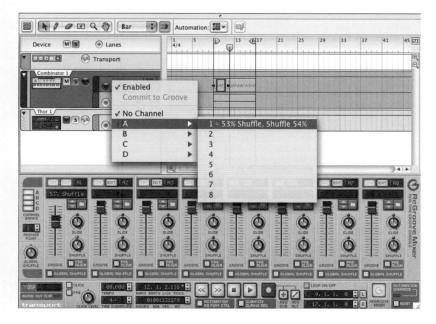

Figure 7.4
Assigning a sequencer lane to a ReGroove Mixer slot.

When you have performed Commit to Groove, the Enabled settings for the affected channels will be set to off.

A particularly important and handy use for ReGroove is in conjunction with the new Sequencer and its lanes. When you are recording a part that may have several elements, for example a ReDrum drum kit or a Combinator part, why not try recording different elements on different lanes? So for example you could set up a loop and record a kick drum part. Then while still recording, add a lane and record the snare part of the loop into a second channel, then the cymbals into a third lane and so on. Then, each individual lane can be routed through a separate ReGroove channel (or several through the same one) in order to get a very specific and human feel to the beats. Quantizing a whole kit with a single setting is something of a blunt instrument now that Reason allows you to tailor the groove, swing and shuffle individually for different sets of notes playing through the same module.

Figure 7.5
A drum part recorded on multiple sequencer lanes and assigned to several ReGroove slots, ensuring a varied and interesting feel for different parts of the kit.

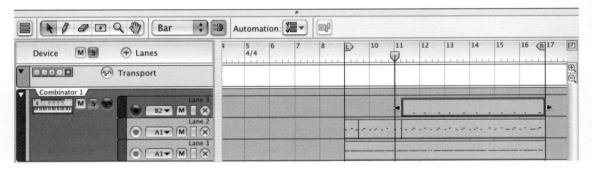

Figure 7.6
Getting the groove from MIDI notes on a sequencer channel.

Tip

Right click on a group of notes and you can choose Get Groove From Clip, which will extract the clip's MIDI timing. This becomes available in the selected ReGroove channel as a patch called User 1, which you can then edit or save.

Some tips for using ReGroove

- Remember that REX files are essentially just MIDI notes triggering sliced audio, so they can be routed through a ReGroove channel just as flexibly as other modules.
- Often, less is more when it comes to groove quantizing. Subtle changes of a few per cent one way or the other can be enough to lend that all

important human feel to a part.

- Timing and velocity settings are different and controlled through the Groove Settings section of the Tool window. If you have a timing that you like but want to experiment with the dynamics, apply the relevant Velocity Impact setting but leave the Timing Impact setting at zero.
- You can apply the same preset or setting to different tracks but in different amounts, using the faders for the ReGroove slots. This is a good way of maintaining the same feel but having a slightly greater or lesser emphasis for certain parts.
- Where you have more than one track or instrument playing the same part, or 'doubling up' the sounds, try offsetting one very slightly using the Random Timing setting in the Tool window after you route it to a ReGroove channel. This will introduce slight random variations into the track's timing, making it seem less like the two have been mechanically aligned by a computer.
- You can apply ReGroove to any data in the sequencer. Try loading up a REX drum loop and placing it into a track. Then, assign it to a new ReGroove slot and solo it. With more complex beats it can be fun to try out some of the MPC patches, taken from AKAI's legendary groovebox series. If you play back as you select patches in the Browser, you'll hear the effects in realtime before you hit OK.
- When extracting the groove from an existing MIDI part, the more timing information it has, the better. So for example a part with lots of notes (or slices if it's a REX file) will make for a better template than one with only a few. Try also to use groups with even lengths like one, two or four bars.
- The ReGroove patches provided on the Sound Bank are a great starting point and in many cases only need small modifications once loaded to sound great in your projects.

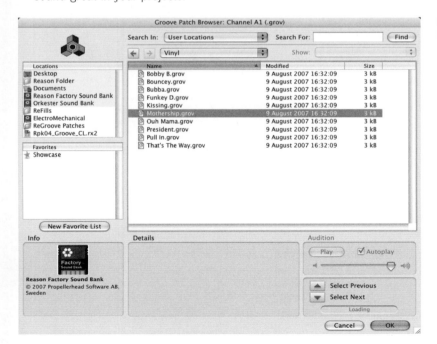

Figure 7.7
Loading a preset ReGroove patch.

Figure 7.8
Access important ReGroove parameters from the Tool window.

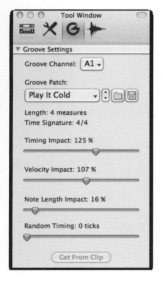

- The new Tool Window contains detailed settings for each ReGroove channel under the Groove Settings tab. Try adding a keyboard part or a beat, then assigning it to a free ReGroove channel and loading a preset like Jade from the Pop-Rock folder. Press the Pre-Align button and then the Edit button on the channel, and go to the Tool Window. The first slider is called Timing Impact and governs the extent to which timing information in the groove template affects the position of the notes. Set at 50%, notes are moved halfway to the position dictated in the template. At 100% they are moved exactly to the position, and at 200% they are moved the same distance again. You can also use the Groove Amount fader to further vary this parameter.

- ReGroove and drums work better together if the drum elements are processed individually. That way you control the feel of each drum separately. Luckily the sequencer now supports multiple note lanes per track, so you can build up a drum part in layers on the same track using the New Dub button on the Transport. Or if you've already recorded the part, create more lanes, duplicate the groups of notes and delete elements from within them selectively so that only one element remains per lane. You can now assign each lane to a different ReGroove channel and use different settings for each, resulting in a much more human and believable feel, especially for parts which are meant to sound acoustic rather than electronic.

- The Shuffle knob adds a sixteenth note swing feel to a channel. Try isolating the hi hats in a drum part and applying a shuffle setting of 66%, and then a slight forward slide to the kick and snare drum parts. Use the Groove Amount faders to determine how much groove between zero and 100% is applied.

Figure 7.9
Save your own ReGroove patches.

- When it comes to attaining a human feel to your MIDI tracks in Reason, less is often more and you should trust your ears, not your eyes. With a little practice using the ReGroove Mixer, you'll wonder how you ever lived without it.

- The ReGroove mixer has 32 slots, four banks A-D on the left times eight visible channels. Move between them using the Bank select buttons A-D. All 32 channels appear in a sequencer lane's dropdown menu, even if no preset is loaded. Of course until a preset is loaded or a setting changed, the routing will have no effect.

Figure 7.10
A project making heavy use of ReGroove, with multiple sequencer lanes routed through many ReGroove slots.

The Combinator

This module, introduced in Reason 3 is a sort of 'shell' within which you can build chains of other devices. It isn't an effect or an instrument, but rather a tool to help you get more out of the other modules. It saves and loads setups in its own file format with the suffix .cmb. Think of it sort of like a rack within the rack. You can have as many Combinators as your CPU can handle, and they come in two basic forms. Instrument combis can contain any combination of instruments, effects and mixers. Effect combis only contain effects units and are used to process rather than generate sound.

Figure 8.1
An instrument combi.

Figure 8.2
An effect combi.

The most obvious applications for the Combinator are threefold. Firstly, for instant recall of instrument / effect combos that you use a lot. Let's say that you have a favourite piano sound with reverb, compression and EQ on it, or a synth patch that sounds great through six Scream boxes. By building it once and saving as a combi patch, it's always available at the click of a button. No more re-building effects chains or copying and pasting from template songs.

Figure 8.3

Info

Create a Combinator by either selecting from the Create menu or by selecting two or more modules in the rack using multiple (shift) select and then selecting Combine from the Edit menu. You can also find this option if you right-click or control-click to bring up the contextual menu with multiple modules selected (Figure 8.4).

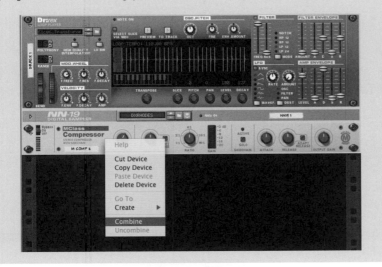

Tip

You can't create a Combinator within another Combinator, or place one inside another by any means! However, if you drag and drop or copy / paste one into another, the devices from the one being copied are uncombined and re-combined within the target Combinator, after its existing modules. Hold shift to ensure auto-routing.

Info

If you choose to create a device by browsing patches you can call any device up from the Browser window. As you browse for Combinator patches, they are loaded so you can play them from the Browser, and information about all modules inside the combi is displayed (Figure 8.5).

Details

Patch Type: Combinator
        Size: 58.84 MB (uncompressed)
    Devices: Line Mixer 6:2, Spider Audio, RV7000, RV7000,
                NN-XT Sampler

Info

If you use the up and down arrow keys on the keyboard you can quickly select different modules in the rack. This takes account of modules within a Combinator, and will 'jump' you inside one when you get to it.

The way to add devices to a Combi is to click in the space at the bottom of it, causing the red insertion line to appear. When this is lit, any device you create will be created inside the combi.

Figure 8.6
The red line means any devices you create will be placed inside the Combinator.

You can drag and drop devices from anywhere in the rack into a combi by dragging their handles – the parts attached to the rack - into the combi. Be aware that when you do this, their original patch connections to the main mixer remain intact. Either manually re-patch them or do the following. As

Figure 8.7
Re-order devices in a combi by dragging their end handles.

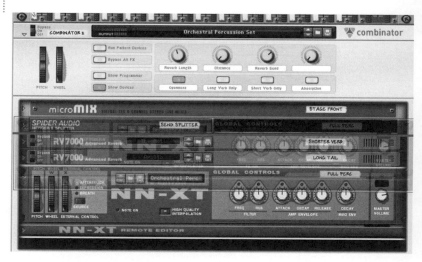

you drag the devices into the combi, hold the shift key and they will be re-routed to inside the combi. If you hold option (Mac) or alt (PC) as you drag the devices, they are copied rather than moved. You can drag devices within a combi to re-order them. The Combinator itself can be moved around the rack like any device.

Tip

Although a Combinator lets you play all the modules within it at the same time, by selecting the Out menu in its sequencer track you can direct MIDI to any of the modules within a combi.

Info

It's fairly essential to create a line mixer or even a ReMix as your first step when making a combi. If you just start to add instruments, only the first instrument will have its outputs sent to the main mixer. If you create a mixer and then add the instruments, their outputs are routed to that mixer, and the summed output is sent to the main mixer. Basically if you don't do this, you'll only hear the output of the first instrument you create! (Figure 8.8)

The second thing the Combinator is good at is making huge sounds. By layering up multiple instruments and effects within a single combi you can play them all at the same time. Layering sounds up in this way it's much easier to create new and massive patches, as big as your CPU will allow. You can for example create lush orchestral sounds by layering up pianos, strings, reverbs and horns all into a single combi. Or, mix different synth modules and effects to create complex electronic sounds.

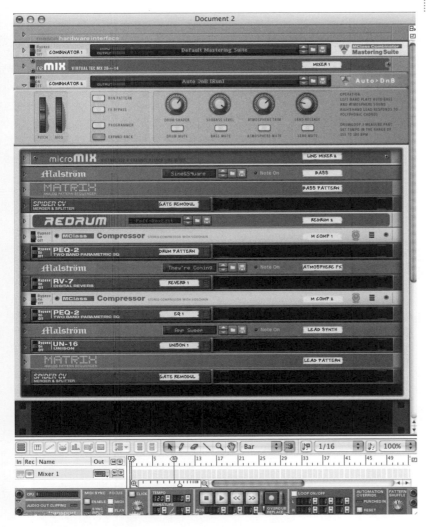

Figure 8.9
Create very complex layered instruments
and manage them easily.

For really cool sounds, you can add pattern devices to a combi (Figure 8.10). So, by adding a Matrix, RPG-8 or a ReDrum and pressing the Run Pattern Devices button, the sequence will play, but only when you press keys. Otherwise it won't make any sound. The sound will be synced to tempo! This is an excellent way of playing arpeggiated sounds and being sure they will stay in time. It also makes you look like a real pro!

In this way, using a couple of control surfaces or keyboards you could do an entire performance without having any data in the main sequencer at all. By further customising the combi and mapping some pads or keys to mutes, pattern changes and so on you can play an entire track, plus variations, from within one Combinator. Remember that each Matrix can store four banks each of eight patterns so there are 32 possible pattern variations within each one. And then remember also that you can have a number of people with controllers locked to separate Combinators, and the vast possibilities for live performance become apparent (Figure 8.11).

Figure 8.10
Use pattern devices within a combi and you can play sequences independently of the main sequencer.

Figure 8.11
Map control devices to a Combinator and get control over the modules within it.

The way to manage combis is by using the programmer window. Press the Show Programmer and Show Devices buttons on the Combinator. For each device within a combi you can assign the four knobs and buttons on the front of the Combinator to perform a different task. Do this by opening the Programmer window, selecting the module you wish to control and then selecting from the list of available controls for rotary knobs 1-4 and buttons 1-4. This is incredibly useful because it means you can make one control do several things at the same time. For example, assigning rotary 1 to control cutoff knobs on four synths will create a sort of master cutoff control, letting you move them all at once. In another example, a button could be made to control multiple effect on/off buttons, letting you punch groups of effects in or out at the same time (Figure 8.12).

Figure 8.12
The programmer window lets you customise the actions of the front panel controls.

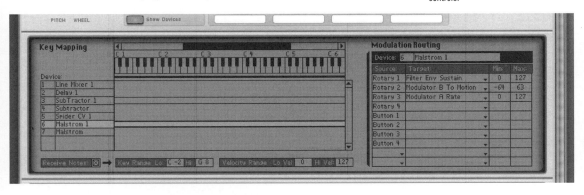

Info

You can rename the controls on the front of a Combinator to make life easier if you have assigned custom actions to them (Figure 8.13).

An easy way to split instruments over the keyboard is to open the combi Programmer window and for each instrument, define a key range. This section is contextual, so you get a different view depending on which instrument you select. Drag the key range slider for each instrument to set its boundaries. Remember, only instruments can be split, not effects.

Figure 8.14
Define key ranges to split sounds over the keyboard.

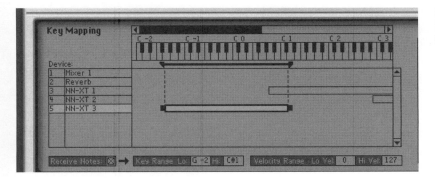

Info

Quickly mute effects within a combi by pressing the Bypass All FX button (Figure 8.15).

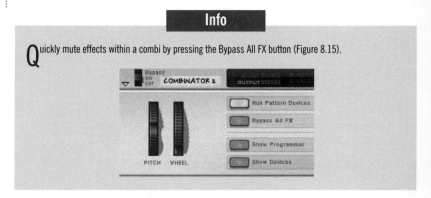

You can use the keyboard to audition selected instrument devices by pressing Option (Mac) or Alt (Windows) and clicking on the keys. This is really useful for playing live. You may for example want to put a bass at the bottom end, piano in the middle and drums at the top of the keyboard. Easy to do by splitting the keyboard into zones. There are some great preset combis included in Reason to try out.

With a little practice and time spent setting up you can build some great combis for instant recall. They are particularly useful for playing live, as you can create custom setups, and then have multiple people playing different Combinators in realtime by locking controllers to them.

Info

By selecting Edit > Select Backdrop with a Combinator selected, or right / control-clicking on it and selecting the same option, you can choose a custom backdrop for the Combinator. This is a first for Reason – you can actually choose any image of your own to use. There are templates supplied – images should be 754x138 pixels and jpeg format. By using the template and changing it in Photoshop you can create your own labels for buttons and any other customisations (Figure 8.16).

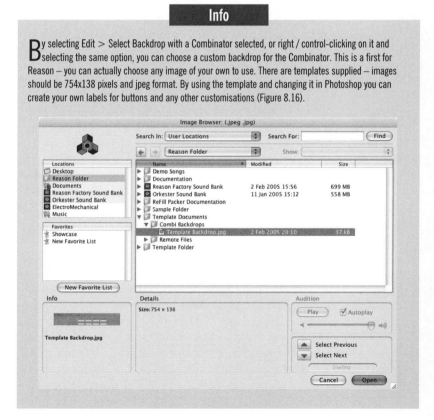

The NN-19 Sampler

When looking at Reason's instruments we're not going to do a blow-by-blow explanation of all the features. That can be found in the manual. Instead we're going to look at things you may not have known, tips for achieving certain common sorts of task and hidden secrets. There's a certain amount of overlap between the workings of many of the instrument modules. For example, the way they load patches, the way synthesis controls work on the synths, filter and envelope sections and so on. For this reason, these will only be mentioned when they are of particular significance to a tip or trick for the instrument in question, and not mentioned once for every module.

Reason doesn't record audio into tracks, but there are certain ways around that. The most obvious are to ReWire it together with another sequencer and to take advantage of the new live sampling features. Previously you would have had to use a wave editor like Peak, Acid, Sound Forge or something similar to record audio in, then cut it to the right length and use it in one of Reason's sampling modules. The NN-19, NN-XT and ReDrum are all able to import audio samples in various formats so you can still do this. The safest bet is to stick with AIFF or WAV files for maximum compatibility, although SoundFont files are supported too.

Like numerous other modules, the NN-19 can now sample directly in using the sampling button on its front panel. Audio routed in through your interface and channels enabled in the Preferences will be captured directly into the NN-19, from where it can be modified and edited. There is, essentially, no further need for an external wave editor. Most Factory NN-19 patches however are still based on collections of pre-recorded samples.

The NN-19 sampler patches that are in the Factory Soundbank contain all the necessary information relevant to that patch. A sampler patch refers to one or more audio files contained within the ReFill. Most sampler patches here are based on multisampled instruments. For example, if you load up a piano in an NN-19, the sampler loads a number of audio samples, probably more than one for each note to account for different velocities (so that playing a key harder or softer will produce different types of sound). It also maps these samples across the keyboard and makes any filter, velocity or envelope settings that have been saved as part of the patch. When you save patches, this information is all stored too.

The NN-19 can be used in three main ways – loading patches or loading samples,or recording your own samples directly in. The file browser button on the left

Figure 9.1
A sampler patch contains links to the audio files plus any other relevant settings.

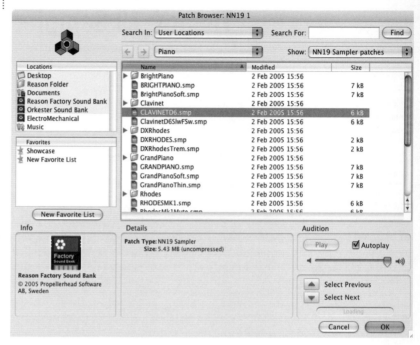

lets you open patches – ready-made instruments, mapped over the keyboard. It also lets you load REX files, which are automatically mapped in sequence over as many keys as the loop has slices. The file browser button in the middle lets you browse for individual audio samples, including those that make up the patches, and also REX files.

You can load any of the individual slices of a REX file into an NN-19.

Figure 9.2
The NN-19 can load sampler patches and individual audio samples.

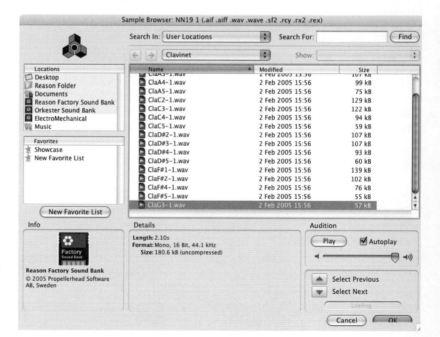

Info

There's an interesting way to make an NN-19 play back a REX loop based on its original form. Load an NN-19 and load the REX loop. Now create a REX player and load the same loop into it. Use its To Track button to place the MIDI notes on its sequencer track. Then drag these notes to the sequencer track for the NN-19 and delete the REX player. The NN-19 will now play the REX loop based on the original REX note data. You MUST load the REX loop into the NN-19 using the patch browser button for this to work. You can multiple-load the slices using the file browser button and repeat this trick for some interesting runs of notes when you paste the sequencer data (Figures 9.3 and 9.4).

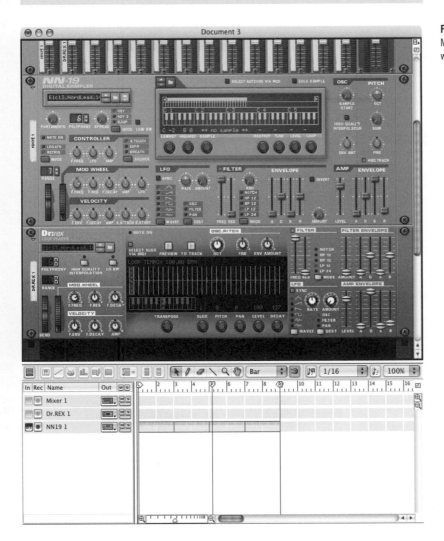

Figure 9.3
Make an NN-19 play back a REX loop with its original rhythm.

Figure 9.4
Load multiple REX slices into the sampler for greater control over individual parts of the loop.

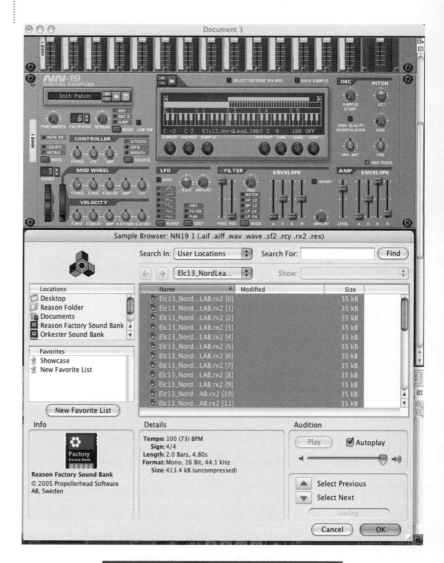

When you have loaded a sample, you can start to alter its parameters using the main window on the NN-19. The whole point about samplers is that you can change the way audio is played back without altering the original audio file on your hard drive. Here is how you could incorporate some of your own recorded material into a Reason song without using ReWire.

Use your own samples – Reason 4 and earlier

Record your sound in a wave editing package. There are lots of cheap and even free ones available. If it is rhythmic in any way, record it to a click track. This is essential for syncing it up later in Reason. You can even use a real metronome, just as long as it's in time. Cut the file into a loop so that it starts and ends at points which allow it to loop perfectly. If the file is a 'hit' and isn't going to be looped, the start point is much more important than the end point.

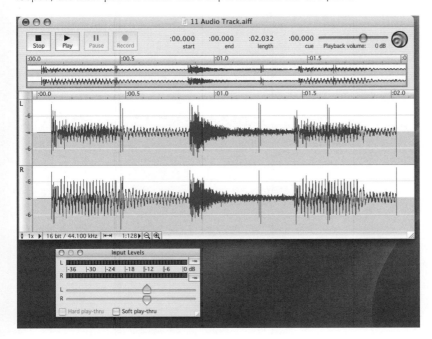

Figure 9.5
Use a wave editing package to record your own audio in in versions prior to 5.

Save the file somewhere, naming it sensibly. Then use the middle file button on an NN-19 to find it and load it. Its root key gets mapped to C3 on your keyboard. This is the key that you press to trigger the sample as it was originally recorded. If you load a single sample, it will be mapped across the entire keyboard. If you play lower and higher keys, the sample will play back at different speeds and pitches.

Figure 9.6
Load individual samples using the file browser button.

Let's say you have loaded a drum loop. If it has been recorded to a click but you don't know its tempo, just activate the click track and attempt to play the sample in time with it. By altering the project's tempo so that the loop plays in time with the click you can make it sync properly. Of course this works best if you don't already have loads of material in the sequencer – if you are using the loop as the starting point for a track rather than adding it to an existing track. If in doubt, set up a four-bar loop and play the sample in once at the start of each bar. Quantize to Bar to make sure it snaps. You could also turn Forward looping on for the sample and just play it once at the very start of the loop. Then, adjust the song's tempo until the loop syncs properly. If your loop hasn't been recorded to a click this step will be very difficult. It also helps greatly if the sample starts at the very beginning of the audio file – if there isn't any silence before the sound comes in.

Figure 9.7
Bring your own loops in and match them to the song's tempo by setting up a loop and changing the tempo until it fits.

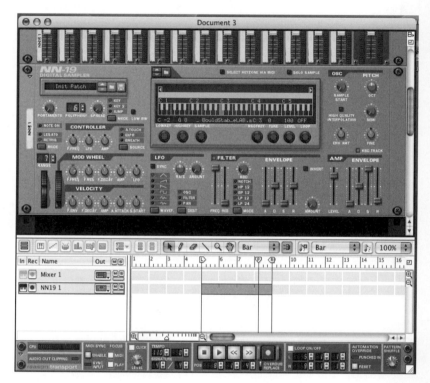

Record the track by holding the key or drawing with the pen tool in the Edit window. Make sure the note starts precisely at the start of a bar. You may need to quantize it to ensure this happens. If your sample is set to loop forwards, you can press the note at the beginning of the bar and then hold it until the end. This will count as one note but will trigger the sample several times. Remember when you play back that in order to trigger the sample the play head must run over the start of the note. If you start it from halfway through the note, nothing will happen.

If you are working with a single hit rather than a loop, you don't need to worry about looping. A popular way of making samples 'stutter' is to play them repeatedly with one finger on the keyboard and end up holding the note so the whole sample plays.

Tip

There are three modes for looping samples – Off, Forward and Forward-Backward. The most useful is Forward. Provided you have created your sample so that it loops seamlessly, you can have your loop playing in sync all the way through the track.

Figure 9.8
Looping forwards is a good way of repeating a sample without it having to be played manually many times.

Info

A really useful way of auditioning samples without using the keyboard is to option (Mac) or alt (PC) click on the keyboard in the NN-19's window and then choose a note (Figure 9.9).

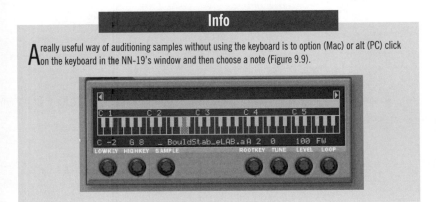

Tip

Samples can be fine-tuned and have their volume altered using the controls under the NN-19's window.

Info

Reason 5 can sample directly in from your audio inputs. Click the waveform icon which denotes the sampling button to open the sampling window. Record your sound in and it is mapped across the keys instantly. Samples can be edited by going to the Tool window's Samples page and selecting your sample, then hitting Edit.

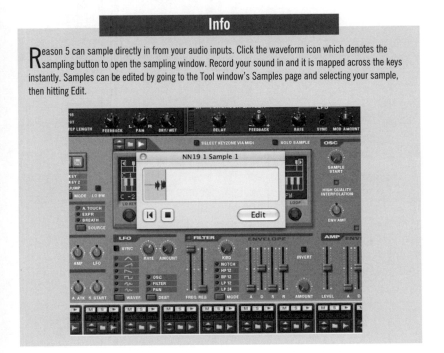

To load several samples into the same sampler, multiple-select them in the browser. Then, by selecting Edit > Split Key Zone you can start to divide the keyboard up into separate zones, which cannot overlap.

Figure 9.10

Figure 9.11

Automapping samples helps to assign them key ranges based on their root key information, if they have it.

Use the Sample knob below to assign each sample to each key zone. You can also pick up the little light blue dividers and drag them around to move the key zones. You can also do this by using the High and Low Key knobs. If your samples contain root key information, you can use the Automap Samples feature from the Edit menu to automatically place all samples in a sampler correctly on the keyboard according to its root note.

There are several other useful things on the front panel of the NN-19 that can help you to be more creative. Here are some ideas.

The Front Panel

The Sample Start knob lets you set a start point for the sample other than the actual start of the file. This can be really useful if, say, there is a breath before a vocal begins, or if there is a glitch at the start of a sound. This control can be used to effectively mute them without changing the sample itself.

Use the Pitch controls to make small or large changes to the sample's pitch. Using the octave control can give you some interesting effects.

The filter controls – especially the frequency slider – are great when you automate them, giving some classic filter sweep effects.

Figures 9.12 and 9.13

You can achieve some really good modulation effects by using the LFO controls on the NN-19. Take a normal sound like a guitar or a piano patch. Then Switch on Sync in the LFO (this is optional but it helps) and raise the amount and rate to somewhere between 50 and 100%. Choose a wave type from the list of six. Now play back. Using the Destination button you can send the mod to osc, filter or pan. Sent to osc, you end up with some cool space effects. A piano is turned into a ray gun sound when you do this. Select filter and provided the filter frequency control is set to something other than full, you get a wah wah or tremelo effect. Set to Pan, you get a nice, almost arpeggiator effect. The results vary depending on the settings you make.

By using the Velocity control section you can make sounds harder or softer. Also, try setting the polyphony to one, then switch the Key Mode to Legato. If you play one note and then play another without releasing the first one, you get an interesting synth-like effect where the subsequent notes have very little attack.

The Voice Spread controls can add a sense of stereo width to your tracks. The three modes will move the pan value of the sound as you play from left to right on the keyboard. Switch polyphony up to be able to play more notes at the same time if you need to.

Figure 9.14
Use the LFO controls to mangle ordinary sounds into totally different ones.

Figure 9.15

Remember that an NN-19 can be played using a Matrix for some interesting sequence effects, just like any other module. It's particularly useful for creating runs of notes or arpeggiated sequences.

Figure 9.16

The Matrix sequencer can play the NN-19 if you enter data into it. This is handy for quickly creating sequences based on samples you have recorded in yourself.

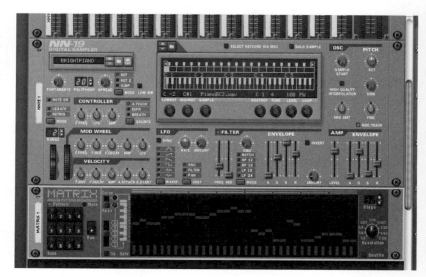

The ReDrum

Modelled partly on vintage, step-based drum machines, the ReDrum combines the strengths of step sequencing with the flexibility of software. That flexibility includes the fact that you can mix and match elements of a drum kit, build your own and automate it just like any other instrument in Reason.

There are several ways to use a ReDrum. By loading patches from the file browser button at the bottom left you can load proprietary .drp patches, which call up drum samples into each of the ten channels on the ReDrum.

Name	Modified	Size
Chemical Kit 01.drp	1/12/2005	7 kB
Chemical Kit 02.drp	1/12/2005	7 kB
Chemical Kit 03.drp	1/12/2005	7 kB
Chemical Kit 04.drp	1/12/2005	7 kB
Chemical Kit 05.drp	1/12/2005	7 kB
Chemical Kit 06.drp	1/12/2005	7 kB
Chemical Kit 07.drp	1/12/2005	7 kB
Chemical Kit 08.drp	1/12/2005	7 kB
Chemical Kit 09.drp	1/12/2005	7 kB
Chemical Kit 10.drp	1/12/2005	7 kB

(Chemical Kits — Show: Redrum patches)

Figure 10.1
Proprietary ReDrum patches.

Or, you can use the file select button on each channel to load any sample you like into each channel, or use teh sampling button located on each channel to manually record sounds directly into that channel. You can mix and match too. Loaded a Reason drum kit but don't like the snare? Change it for one of your own by using the browser or sampler on that particular channel. In fact, there's nothing to stop you loading ten snares into a module and just playing those. Or eight horn stabs and a cymbal – it's up to you (Figure 10.2).

Each channel has its own set of audio controls. This means you can edit the sound of each constituent part of your drum loop. For example, the bass drum might need to be lowered in pitch and raised in volume. Or the hats might need panning. All this can be done without affecting the other channels in the ReDrum. This is also interesting if you load a REX file into a ReDrum. By loading the slices

Figure 10.2
Use your own samples in any ReDrum channel. They don't have to be drum samples if you don't want them to be.

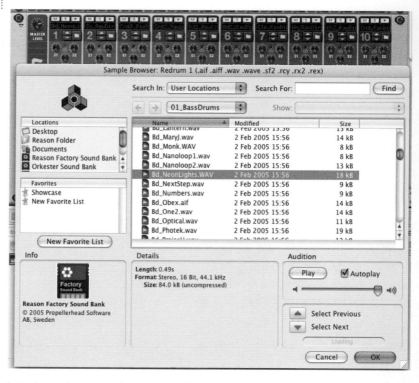

You don't have to load drum samples into the ReDrum. Try loading sound fx or instrument hits, mixing and matching kits and effects in the channels. When you play them back from the keyboard you'll get some weird and wonderful results.

Tip

Create totally original kits by sampling live straight into a Redrum's channels. Make a beatbox kit or a junk kit by recording and editing short samples and then playing them either with a keyboard or the onboard pattern sequencer.

into channels separately you can gain control over the sound of each slice really easily and then assemble them into entirely new patterns. The sound loaded into each channel can be auditioned, muted or soloed by using the three buttons at the very top of it. It's also easy to make drum sounds snappier by reducing their length using the Length knob.

Figure 10.3
Each channel has independent audio controls

Info

By using the Level and Velocity controls on each drum channel you can effectively sub-mix a kit before it is sent to the mixer. This saves you having to try to even out the drums too much with compressors and EQ. There's also a Master Level control at the top left.

Each channel has two effect send knobs near the top of it, corresponding to the first two send effects attached to the main mixer. Using these is a good way of effecting parts of a drum pattern but not others. For example, applying reverb to the snare but not the bass drum. You can even apply effects only to certain snare beats (for example) by having the same snare loaded into two channels, one playing most of the way through the pattern but the second playing periodically and through the effect.

Figure 10.4
Effect drum kit elements separately using the effects sends on each channel

Figure 10.4a
Sampling directly into a ReDrum channel in Reason 5.

Step recording

The two record modes – step and normal sequencer – are covered in detail in the manual. However there are some useful tricks to be found when recording.

Everything is contextual, so the drum channel that is selected is the one that will be controlled by the 16 step buttons. The Select button lights up for the active channel, and only one can be selected at once.

You can switch each pattern up to a total of 64 steps. If you go beyond 16, you have to use the Edit Steps switch to make the visible step buttons correspond to the additional steps beyond 16 that you have added. You can of course shorten a pattern, in which case any steps programmed after will simply not play back.

Figure 10.5

Figure 10.6
Work with up to 64 steps, using the Edit
Steps knob to access them all.

If you're working in step mode you have to have the Enable Pattern Section
button activated. Use the Run control to stop and start patterns. You can play
the ReDrum patterns without ever actually starting the main sequencer, as it has
its own sequencer in it. When you use the pattern select buttons and banks to

Figure 10.7
Press a ReDrum Run button and hear it
without starting the main sequencer.

choose new patterns, Reason waits until the current one has finished playing
before moving on to the next. This is great for playing it live as it means you can
flip between patterns without fear of slipping out of sync.

Each step can have a hard, medium or soft dynamic applied to it to create
more natural variations in the dynamics of a pattern. Either select the step and
alter the setting, or hold down shift while clicking to apply a hard dynamic.

The Shuffle control will introduce a more natural 'swing' to the pattern.
The amount of swing is set globally, using the Pattern Shuffle knob on the
Transport Panel. Use with care, as it can often wildly change the feel of a pat-
tern, and not always for the better.

Figure 10.8

The Resolution control lets you alter the subdivisions of beats to which the ReDrum is locked. 1/16 is the normal setting. 1/32 can be good for Drum and Bass, and other settings like 1/64 or 1/128

Figure 10.9
Alter the resolution to create more complex patterns.

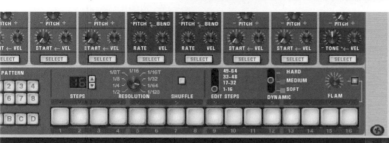

Figure 10.10
The Flam control helps to create doubled-up drum effects.

let you program drum rolls and fills. The more precise the resolution, the more intricate the beats you can program.

You can simulate double drum hits by using the Flam control. Activate Flam and then set the amount and click the LED above each step you want to have flam. A little usually works better than a lot, and it will take a bit of practice to get it sounding really natural. This is also a good way of creating double bass drum kicks, very close together.

Here is a good way of creating a convincing snare 'double hit'. Identify the snare beat you want and then insert another one directly before it, with its dynamic set to soft. Then apply a Flam value of around 55 to that quieter snare hit. Voila... a short drum fill.

Each of the ten channels on the ReDrum has a separate audio L and R out, as well as CV in and out. This makes it incredibly versatile. Although you might normally just send the summed stereo

Figure 10.11
Route some or all of the ten drum channels out and process them independently, for amazing versatility.

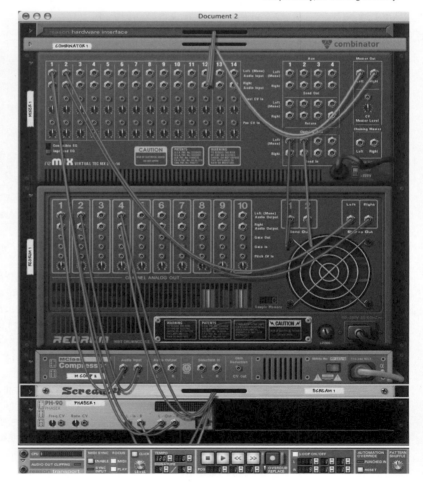

Figure 10.12

output to the mixer, you can separate off some or all of the channels and process them independently. Imagine – you could build amazing drum kits by sending each channel to a separate mixer channel, where you apply different effects, pan and automated levels to each one. If you use up every channel on one ReMix, just create another.

A good way to create stereo space in a ReDrum is to duplicate, say, a hi-hat track and pan one channel left and one right.

The Edit menu gains some useful items when you select a ReDrum. There are a multitude of ways to modify the patterns you create, which saves you time programming variations. The most useful are :

• Cut, Copy, Paste and Clear pattern. Save time when varying patterns by copying and pasting patterns to a new slot and making minor changes.
• Shift Pattern and Shift Drum. These move notes for a pattern or drum channel to the left or right. Again, great for creating variations.
• Randomize Pattern and Drum will create a totally new arrangement for either the whole pattern or just the selected drum channel. Variations, here we come!
• Alter Pattern and Drum make changes by re-allocating the current notes to the drum sounds at random. This is less chaotic than simply randomizing them.

Info

There's an interesting feature whereby if you select Channel 8&9 Exclusive on a ReDrum, the sound from one will automatically silence the other. This is useful for tasks like making sure an open hi-hat cuts of a closed one, as you get in real life.

Tip

You will find that keys C2 to E3 on your keyboard actually mute the drum channels on a ReDrum. This is an interesting way of creating drum patterns – by having loads of drum hits playing, and selectively muting them on the fly by using the keyboard. The results are usually chaotic...

Sequencer recording

If you deactivate the Enable Pattern Section button, the ReDrum works like a normal sound module and you can play notes in by hand from the MIDI keyboard. Again, this is best done to a click track and quantized afterwards. If you have recorded a drum pattern in step mode you can convert it to MIDI notes by selecting the required pattern on the ReDrum and choosing Copy Pattern to Track.

The notes will then be inserted between the left and right locators. This works for any pattern you select, but be aware that if you try to copy more than one pattern to the same area on the sequencer, both sets of notes will co-exist at the same point, which can get very cluttered. One upside of copying notes like this is that it gives you a much clearer view of what's being played.

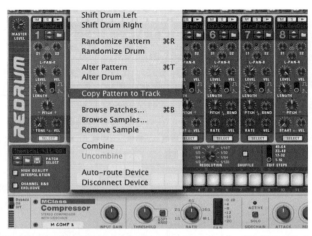

Figure 10.13

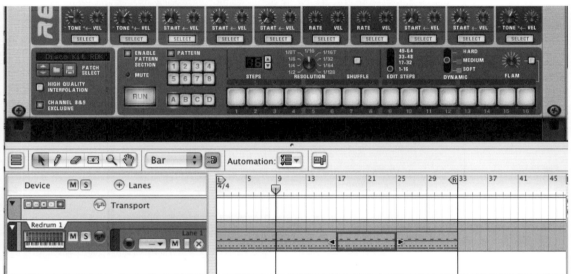

Notes can be placed in the Key lane, Drum lane and REX lane for a ReDrum, which gets a bit busy sometimes. If you have recorded some patterns using step mode, a good way to put those into the sequencer is using the Pattern lane. Here are some things to know about programming patterns in the sequencer.

Figure 10.14
Copy drum patterns to the sequencer from the ReDrum.

Pattern programming

The pattern lane works with blocks of information, not notes. It's a good idea to use the dropdown pattern selector to enter the default pattern for the device, as when you start to insert data it will fill the whole lane with that value until you change it. Setting the snap value to Bar is also a good idea unless you're dealing with unusual pattern changes mid-bar.

Figure 10.15
The Pattern Lane
works with blocks
of data, not notes.

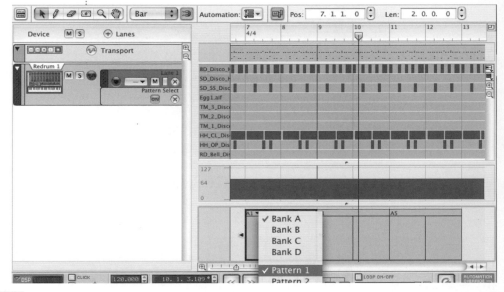

Figure 10.16

You have to draw data in with the pencil tool. Reason will associate the new data you draw with whichever pattern you select from the menu. Obviously you should only select patterns that contain notes, unless you want the ReDrum to drop out for a few bars, in which case you can select an empty one.

Copy, paste and delete pattern change data by drawing around it with the pointer tool and using the familiar Edit menu commands. When pattern selection has been automated in this way, the ReDrum gets a green box around its pattern select buttons.

Figure 10.17
Making a ReDrum channel trigger a
sampler note.

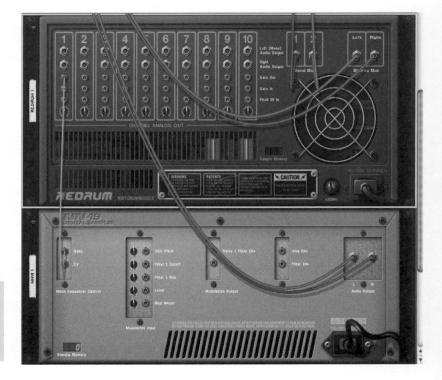

Tip

If you connect the Gate output of one ReDrum channel to the Gate in on another, you can play both channels from the same key.

Here's an interesting way of using Gate CV out from a ReDrum channel to control another device. Take the Gate CV out from a channel on the ReDrum that contains a bass or snare sound. Connect it to the Mono Sequencer Control Gate input on an NN-19, with, say, a piano loaded. Now the drum sound will play a note on the NN-19. Alter the note it plays using the Octave or Semi control on the sampler. This sort of musical trick is used a lot in reggae or hip hop, where a guitar chord might have to play along with a snare beat. Use this method rather than trying to copy and duplicate notes. It ensures that for every drum hit made by that ReDrum channel, the instrument in question will be played too.

Kong Drum Designer

Kong Drum Designer is a multi-talented drum synthesizer with nine drum modules to choose from featuring analog synthesis, physical modeling, sampling, REX loops, support sound generators, effects, flexible routing and multiple hit types on its 16 pads. The perfect partner for ReDrum, Kong allows you to change the way your drum hits are synthesized rather than just using samples, and so is capable of much more advanced sound sculpting. Each pad is assigned to a module and can also use its own effects including delays, reverbs, ring modulation, transient shaping, compressors and filters so it's easy to build amazing sounding kits really quickly. With the NN-Nano sampler you can record your own sounds to use as part of a kit, and also use the Nurse REX player to incorporate REX loops and slices. Kong is what Reason has been needing for a while – a really powerful, flexible drum synthesizer and sampler, and if you get bored of the great presets it's fun to customize as well.

How does it work?

Kong's interface is very accessible if you just want to start playing immediately. It doesn't have the ReDrum's step sequencer built in, because this is called a drum 'designer', whereas ReDum is a drum 'computer'. The emphasis here is on creating kits, though you can of course use MIDI parts from other sources to trigger it as well as playing it by hand from a keyboard. It loads kits in its own format, and like other modules you can save your own patches. In the main interface there's quite a lot you can do in terms of changing the sounds. Select a pad and then in the display window, you get a range of controls to change its tone, pan, level and pitch settings, plus bus and aux send effect controls. If you click on the sample name you can also reassign the sound source, if the pad is triggering an audio sample.

Figure 11.1
Kong's display can be used to quickly access alternate samples.

What is Q for?

You will see a number of Q buttons on the front panel and when clicked, these will reveal a Quick Edit view for each of the 16 pads. So for example if you click on the Q button by the Level knob, you can drag the markers to alter the tone and level of the sound associated with each pad. All 16 can have different values if you like. The same goes for pan and level, effect send and pitch.

Figure 11.2
Quickly make parameter changes across any of the pads using the Quick Edit buttons.

Figure 11.3
Combine mute automation with Kong to control your kit in realtime.

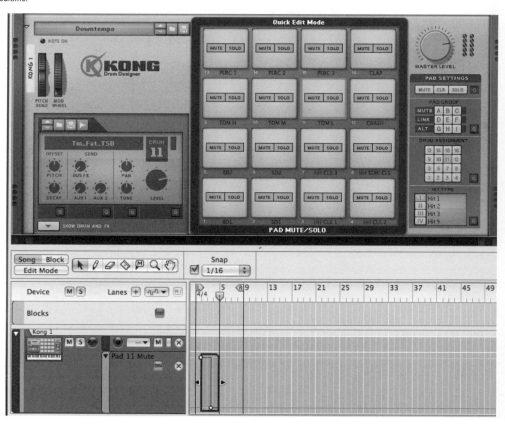

You also get Quick Edit buttons on the Pad controls, and these have a number of uses. Pad Settings can be used to mute or solo specific pads within a kit. This is useful when combined with automation, because it means you can have certain pads inactive at specific points, but then come to life when you want them. Imagine in a live situation you didn't want a pad to accidentally be triggered until a certain point in the song – this would be the way to do it.

A similar theory applies to Pad Groups, the next item down. You can link pads together in groups so that pressing one also triggers another. This is handy when playing live because it means you can use a single finger to play two or more pads. The Alt command here is also useful because it means that any pad assigned as an 'alt' to the pad you hit will be played on every second hit. So the pad you're pressing sounds every time but pads linked to it using alt sound only every second press. This is handy for triggering a hi hat alternately to a kick drum for example, a common dance music trick.

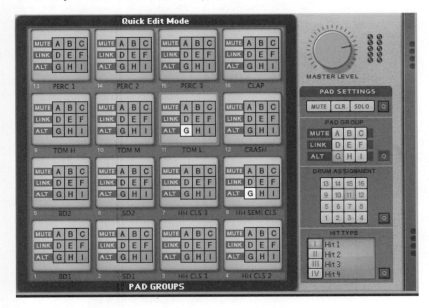

Figure 11.4
Use Pad groups to creatively control and play Kong in a live environment.

Drum assignment is the next section, and here you get to assign a pad to play a drum sample or module that is assigned to a different pad. This might be something you don't use all that often, but it's good to know it's there. Finally there are Hit Types that you can assign to pads, again with Quick Edit control for speedy assignment. Some drum sounds, particularly things like hi hats, have more than one hit type. In that example it would be open and closed. You can change the way these kinds of sounds are produced by changing their hit type, though not every drum part has more than one so if it doesn't, you will not notice a change.

The Editor

The really interesting stuff in Kong happens when you expand the Drum and

FX section, which you could also call the Editor section since it's where the sounds are generated. For each pad that you select you will see a number of modules appear and these determine the way that pad makes its sound. The NN-Nano sampler is a small version of the NN-XT whicih supports both live sampling and up to four different sample layers, with a split function and velocity. It also supports live sampling and the editing of existing samples, via the Edit Sample button. The NN-Nano is how Kong works with conventional audio samples, and provides a surprising amount of flexibility in morphing and editing them. This is all, remember, for a single drum pad.

Figure 11.5
The NN-Nano module provides live sampling straight into a Kong kit.

You can click the tiny Drum Module icon at the top left of an editor section in Kong to select an alternative model. The Nurse REX is an interesting little module that allows the loading of REX files and editing of the way they play back. Slices can be pitched or turned up and down and you can select a range of slices to be played, so you can play back bits of a loop rather than the whole thing. Hit a pad and the loop will play. This is a good way to play multiple loops within a single kit, or combine loops with regular drum hits.

Figure 11.6
The Nurse REX can load whole REX loops into a Kong pad.

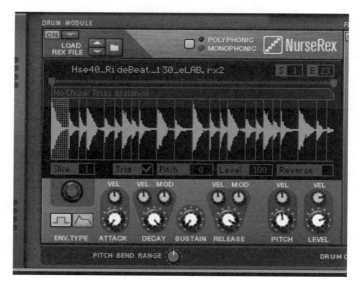

The remaining modules are split into two broad categories – physical and synth. The physical bass, snare and tom modules can be tuned, their physical sizes changed and the tone and velocity of the stick they are played with

Figure 11.7
Physical drum modelling in Kong.

all changed by the user. You are encouraged to play with these, since they can really help you to tweak the sound and get it just how you want it. These are modelled on real drums. The Synth options however are not, and these recreate classic drum machine sounds. The controls on offer let you tweak the way the sound is synthesized, so again you can tune and shape them easily.

Figure 11.8
Synth drum modules in Kong.

Effects in Kong

Each pad, as well as having a generator, can have two insert effects applied to it. Over the course of a whole kit, this means that there's the potential to use lots of effects to tailor the sound of the drums. These are fairly self explanatory, ranging from EQ and compression to overdrive and echo. Some crunch and compression can beef up a weaker sound, and some echo and reverb can give you a nice dub sound. The effects are fun to play with, and there are also bus and master fx, which apply to all channels. Apply Bus effects on a per-pad basis in the main display and the aux sends by default go to the effects attached to the main mixer in the project. So as well as applying effects to each pad you can use master, bus and aux effects to colour the sound.

Figure 11.9
Use multiple types of effects to sweeten your sound within Kong.

A note about routing

Kong defaults to stereo but can use multiple outputs – one for each pad / generator in fact. At the base of the unit you will see the option to route any drum to a range of available outputs.

Figure 11.10
Assign different drum modules to different physical outputs.

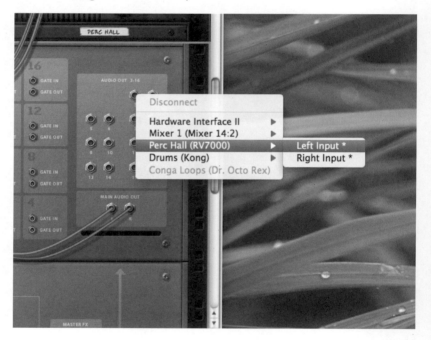

If you spin the rack around (Figure 11.11) you will see that Kong has numerous ports. The audio outs can be used to route drum channels flexibly, and there's sequencer control in as well. Each pad has independent CV gate in and out, so that drum patterns can be controlled from other devices and can in turn control other devices. Along the bottom you will see that it also supports audio input, for using it as an effect processor. You can even use Kong to process external audio sources from other modules and continue to use it as a regular drum machine as well.

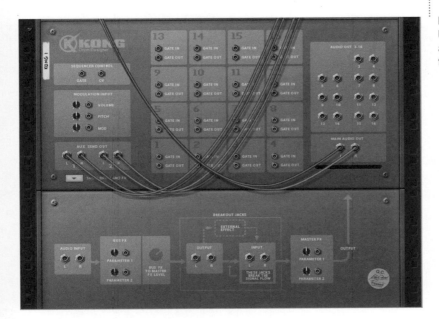

Figure 11.11
Use Kong to flexibly route audio out, and also as an effect device to process audio from other modules.

An example of programming with Kong

- Set up a loop and activate the click track, then record a basic pattern, say just a kick and snare using Kong. You can either do this by playing the MIDI notes in from your keyboard or control surface, or by playing the pads on Kong's interface with the mouse. For the ultimate in tactile control you might try locking a MIDI pad controller to Kong using the Remote system, making it even more hands-on. Once you are done you may wish to quantize the part you just recorded.
- You have the option of substituting pads quickly to try out different sounds. If you select a pad in Kong and then click on an alternative box in the Drum Assignment box to the right, you can assign a new sound to that pad, changing the sound of the beat without having to reassign any MIDI notes. Just think of it as swapping the sounds around in their slots.
- By clicking on the Show Drum and FX arrow you can reveal the generators that are creating the sounds and tinker with them if you like, plus add and edit effects. Sometimes the hits are based on sampled sounds, but you can change these – even sample directly in if you like into the NN-Nano samplers. Try swapping one of the sounds for a synthesized hit by clicking on its source select arrow.
- Tweak its controls until it sounds good to your ears. Activate one or more of the FX units to add some interest. You can do this independently for every pad on Kong, and there are bus and master FX available as well. Try adding a Rattler to a snare sound, for example.
- Next, try duplicating the simple MIDI part you have recorded and adding a couple more hits to it using either the MIDI key editor or just by hitting record and playing the pads or MIDI keys. To differentiate the clip from others you can right click on it and choose to assign it a new colour, which makes things easier to keep track of.

Tip

Right click on any drum pad in Kong to copy and paste settings quickly between pads.

Tip

Kong can use custom backdrops and you can assign and manage these from the Edit menu when Kong is selected.

Tip

Select Kong and choose Edit > Manage Samples to see a list of all samples currently in use.

The Dr:Rex Player

REX loops are created by ReCycle, another of Propellerheads' creations. It works by analyzing an audio file and slicing it up into many small parts. The exported REX file can then have its tempo and pitch altered drastically without the side effects that can occur when you timestretch or pitch shift a loop normally. The easiest way to use REX files in Reason is with the Dr:Rex player. Here are some things to know about it.

Working with the Dr:Rex

You can preview REX files from the browser in Reason, just like you can with any patch or sound. However you can also load a REX file and audition it without having to place any information on a sequencer track. Just use the Preview button on the Dr:Rex. The loop will automatically adapt to the tempo of your song, regardless of what tempo the loop starts off at.

Figure 12.1
Preview a loop before you place it into the sequencer.

The main window on the Dr:Rex provides a good way of editing the slices in a loop before you copy it to the sequencer. Each of the slices can be seen, divided by red lines. You can select any of the slices and the pitch, pan, level and decay controls under the window will alter that particular slice. Let's say you have a drum loop and you want one of the snare hits to be louder and higher. Identify its slice by alt (Mac) or control (PC) clicking on the slice to audition it. Then alter the controls accordingly. Use the Preview button to hear the loop play.

Figure 12.2
You can edit slices independently from the Slice window

You can also move between the slices using the Slice knob. The transpose knob to the left will transpose the entire loop without changing the tempo. This is a good way of matching musical loops to the key of your song. You can use the small keyboard on the window to alter the root key of the loop as well.

Figure 12.3

A REX loop must be copied to its sequencer track before it fully becomes part of the song. However if you play the song and hit the preview button, loops will audition in sync, which helps you see if they're going to work or

Figure 12.4
There are several ways of getting REX data into the sequencer.

not. To copy REX notes to the sequencer, press the To Track button on the Dr:Rex. Alternatively, select Edit > Copy REX Loop to Track. In both cases the loop will be copied between the left and right locators regardless of how far apart they are.

It is quite possible to play a REX file from the keyboard, treating it essentially as a set of samples. This can be a really interesting way of creating entirely new patterns out of an existing loop. It could be that you love the snare and bass drum sounds in a loop, but don't like the pattern they play. In this case, simply make sure MIDI is directed at the Dr:Rex, then play and record the sequencer while you play the slices in their new pattern from the keyboard. Remember that slices correspond to sequential parts of the loop, not always separate sounds. You may find that the same basic snare sound is triggered from three different keys, or that certain keys trigger slices that contain an entire fill, or a cymbal and a kick drum. This is one of the strengths

Tip

To create a large number of instances of a REX loop, rather than copying and pasting, when you press To Track, just make sure the left and right locators are set suitably far apart.

Tip

The Octave and Fine controls can be used to transpose and tune a loop before it is assigned to a sequencer track. Also, if you switch on Select Slice Via MIDI, you can use keyboard keys to automatically select slices in the Dr:Rex.

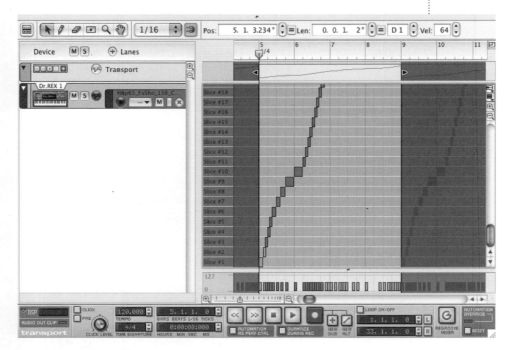

of re-building loops in this way – you can create some great new patterns with relatively little effort.

Another way of doing this would be to make sure the MIDI notes were in the sequencer, then select them and use Edit > Change Events to introduce some randomization.

Figure 12.5
Play a REX loop from the keyboard like it was an instrument.

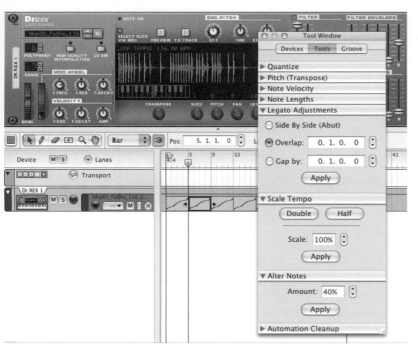

Figure 12.6
Change Events and other editing tools for notes are now found in the Tool Window.

Yet another way would be to drag the note data from another instrument's sequencer track to the Dr:Rex's sequencer track. If you do this, remember that the Dr:Rex only responds to as many notes as the loop has slices, so any notes above or below that range won't trigger any sounds. REX files can have over 90 slices, but in practice they don't tend to have more than 20 or 30 maximum.

Figure 12.7
Copy notes from other instruments' tracks to make them play the Dr:Rex.

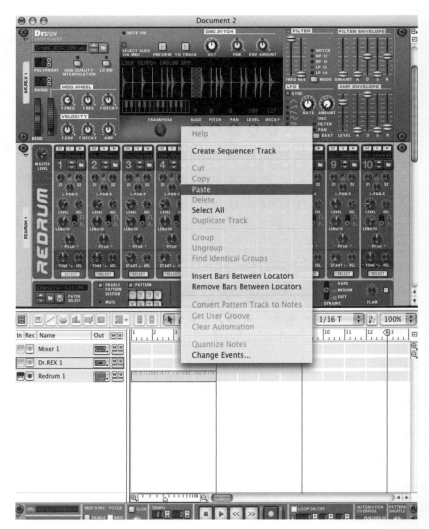

Once notes are in the sequencer there are other ways of messing with them. The most obvious is to enter Edit mode, activate the REX lane or key lane and start to re-arrange notes by hand. Hovering the mouse over the Slice numbers or keys and clicking will audition the slices, and the notes can be edited, lengthened / shortened, moved, duplicated or removed just like any other notes. If you quantize the loop you can impose different timings on it. If you transpose it by transposing the MIDI notes (Edit > Change Events) the pitch won't alter but rather the notes will be shifted up or down the grid, meaning they play back in a totally new pattern.

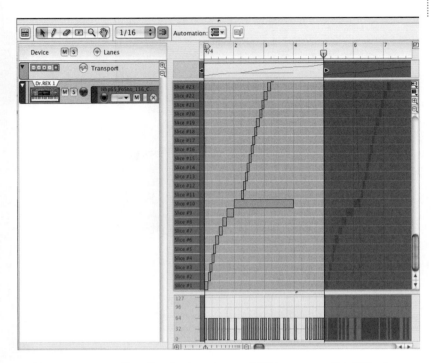

Figure 12.8
Use the REX or Key lanes to manually
edit notes. Add, remove or change them.

Here are some other tips for how to use REX loops and the REX player.

If you don't want to use drum loops that are obviously sampled, try this. Do the majority of your drum programming in a ReDrum so the patterns are uniquely yours. Then find a REX loop that 'enhances' or backs up the main rhythm. Load it and adjust its volume so that it complements your drums rather than overpowering them. You may have to use the filters on the Dr:Rex to drop most of the bass and some of the mid out of the loop so that it sits behind the main drum rather than competing with it. Also, try using an EQ module to make the REX pattern sit better behind the main drum (Figure 12.9).

Like most of the other instruments, the Dr:Rex has CV ins and outs, and so can be used as a modulation source, or modulated by other sources. Here's an example. Load a Dr:Rex and put a drum loop in it. Copy the notes to the sequencer. Now create a Matrix sequencer with some note data in it and connect its Gate CV out to the Amp Env Gate in on the Dr:Rex. You should get a real cut-up effect on the drums. If you activate Shuffle on the Matrix, you get more of a groove effect (Figure 12.10).

Here's another good way to create some new REX patterns. Load up a Dr:Rex and load a drum or instrument loop. Create a Matrix and enter some data into it. Now connect the Matrix's Note CV out to the OSC Pitch CV input on the Dr:Rex, switching the knob up to full. Spin the rack around and switch the Dr:Rex's octave control all the way to the left. Now, the data you enter in the Matrix will control the pitch of the loop, with some interesting results! Try moving the knob on the OSC pitch input to the centre position for a more trippy sound.

One of the strengths of REX loops is the particular feel that they can have. Even if you don't like a loop's sound, you can still capture its timing. With

Tip

To give REX parts a more human feel, route their sequencer tracks through the ReGroove mixer and alter the shuffle and swing nondestructively.

Figure 12.9
Use REX loops as rhythm enhancers rather than main beats, to avoid an obviously looped feel to your drums. Take advantage of the ReGroove mixer to apply the same swing to multiple beats.

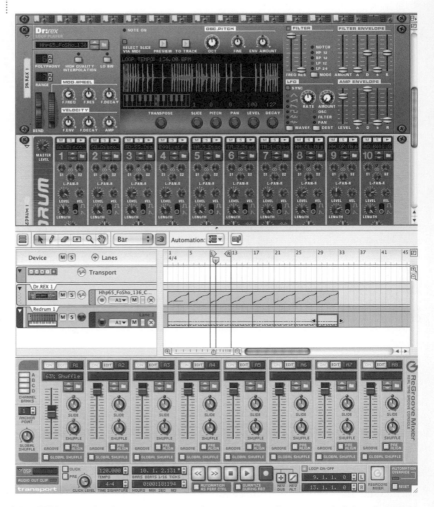

the REX notes in the sequencer, select a group of notes and right-click (PC) or control+ click (Mac) on them and select Get User Groove. This makes the unique timing of that loop available in the quantize menu for you to apply to

Figure 12.10
Use a Matrix with CV connected to a Dr:Rex for cut-up drum effects.

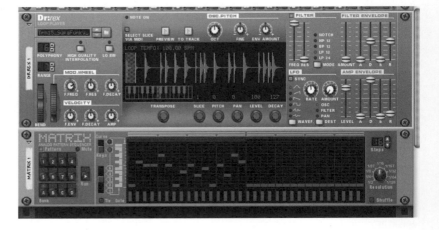

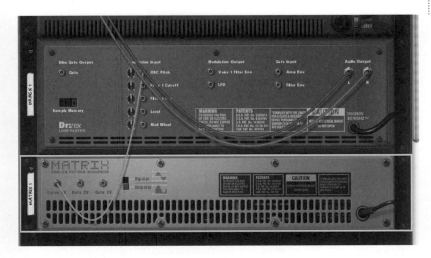

Figure 12.11
Connect the Curve out of the Matrix to the OSC Pitch in for some cool filter sweeps.

other notes. This is really useful for getting a more natural and less mechanical feel to your tracks.

A good way of working with sampled loops in the Dr:Rex is to play with the filter section. It's a little predictable, but drum loops do sound good with automated cutoff and filter sweeps! A lot of REX files tend to be in mono, so to increase their stereo width you can switch on the LFO and sync control, choose a waveform and switch the destination to Pan. Remember also to turn up the rate and amount knobs. Get a wah wah effect on the drums by switching the destination to Filter.

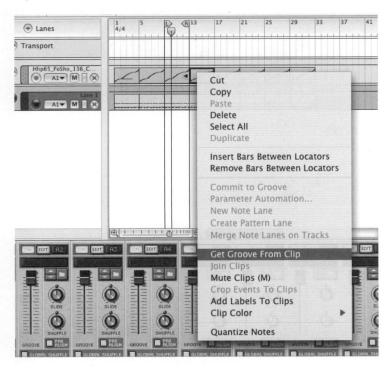

Figure 12.12
Extract the groove from a REX loop and use it to quantize other parts.

Tip

Sharpen up your drum loops by moving the decay slider in the Amp section towards the bottom.

Figure 12.14
Put several REX players inside a Combinator. By playing and recording the Combinator, you control all the modules inside it at the same time.

Info

A good way of getting control over several REX players at the same time is to put them inside a Combinator. Then you can attach effects, Matrix sequencers and make some unique patterns by drawing in the REX lane for the Combinator and controlling multiple REX players. The results will also only use up a single channel in the main mixer.

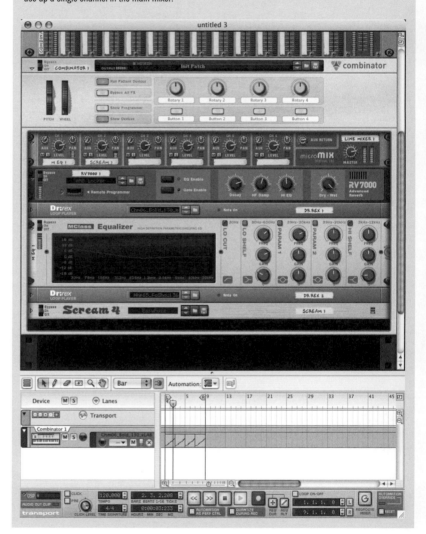

Dr Octo Rex

What is it?

The Dr:Rex loop player that debuted in Reason version 1 was a breath of fresh air for musicians, finally providing a friendly front end for Rex loops. The Rex format had also been developed by Propellerhead and while you had been able to create and use such loops for a while, nothing had even approached the simplicity of the Dr Rex for sheer speed and utility. It was great, letting you drop loops into any project and have them automatically time stretch, quickly building ideas or backing tracks with just a few clicks. As Reason matured however, the Dr Rex remained largely static, experiencing few if any real modifications over the years. That's all changed in Reason 5, where as part of a major overhaul, one particular drawback that many people found with Dr:Rex has been addressed.

The great thing about Rex loops is that they slot easily into any project and as such, are a good way to build backing tracks, whether for jamming ideas over or when actually writing a piece of music. The problem was that the Dr Rex could only hold one loop at a time so if you wanted to use a series of loops from the same collection, say, a drum part with intros, verses, choruses and breakdowns for example, you needed one module per loop. This wasn't a huge problem, but it was cumbersome and could quickly result in the rack and sequencer becoming cluttered with Rex devices. The name of the new module, the Dr Octo Rex, may give you a hint as to one of the ways in which it has changed. Each one can now hold up to eight loops at once, and the sequencer can be programmed to play them back in whatever order you like. It's not limited to waiting for one to finish before the next starts either, so you can be truly creative with it. This new approach makes the module more suitable than ever for building song structures quickly and easily without having to load up endless rack modules.

The basics of Dr Octo Rex are pretty straightforward in that you load up to eight REX loops into its eight slots. The resulting patch can be saved and

Tip

If you load up a project from an older version of Reason, any Dr REX modules will be automatically converted to Dr Octo Rex modules, containing just a single loop.

Figure 13.1
Load up to eight REX loops in a single module and sequence them in the sequencer.

recalled, and there's a trigger control to govern how it handles the transition from one loop to the next – next bar, next beat or next 1/16 measure.

Into the details

If you load up a new Dr Octo Rex, you will see that its design has changed substantially. In the Factory Sound Bank there is now a new folder called Dr Octo Rex Patches and inside this, multiple patches with the suffix .drex. These are patches that contain information about which of the eight slots will be occupied, and with which loops. Try loading one up, click a numbered button to choose a loop and then hit the Run button on the module to play it back. Of course the loops will play back at whatever tempo your project is so you may want to change the project tempo. As it plays back, try clicking one of the other slots and you will find that as the current loop ends, the next one begins. This is the default behaviour and it's the 'safest' way to use the module, in the sense that even if you press a button halfway through a loop, it won't suddenly jump to the next loop and go out of time.

In some cases though you may well want to flip between loops at a more precise point instead of at the end – say for example on the next beat. This kind of thing can sound great when you're either doing a live performance or creating hip hop or cut-up music, to quickly make very varied beats. Luckily, there's a simple way to do this here. At the top left of the module you will see a section called 'Trig Next Loop' and this controls whether the next loop will wait for the end of the current one, wait for the next beat or wait only one sixteenth of a beat, which is more or less instantaneous. Needless to say if you set this to 1/16 you will need to have pretty nimble fingers if you're doing it manually.

Playing a series of loops live is cool, and you can even trigger each slice of each loop manually by playing it from your MIDI keyboard, just like you could before, only now you can direct the MIDI to any of the eight slots to re-sequence loops on the fly. Much of the time though, you will probably want to program the Dr Octo Rex to play back a series of loops in a specific order. This would be the way to build a structure to form the basis of a song, and there are a number of ways to do it. The first is to program the module in the way you may be familiar with, by placing loops onto the sequencer track. If you select a loop, expand the module's programmer section and then click the Copy Loop to Track button, that loop will be placed onto the Octo Rex's sequencer track in the area between the left and right locators. If you then move the markers to another area, select a new loop slot and repeat the process, that loop will be placed in the same way. By doing this you can build up a backing track in a conventional manner, using MIDI clips in the sequencer. These are easy to copy, delete and move as normal. The only caveat with this method is that when playing back you must deactivate Enable Loop Playback on the module, or the loops will play two at once.

The second method for programming the Dr Octo Rex is to automate the slot playback order, and this can be done in a couple of ways. The quickest is to select the sequencer track and press record, making sure Enable Loop Playback is switched on. As the track plays back, simply press the button of the slot you want to play back. You can also change the trigger behaviour on the fly as well, though this isn't recorded as automation. What happens is that the Pattern Select lane is populated based on your choices. By clicking on the arrow next to the number on each block, you are able to select a new loop to play back in that section, if you change your mind afterwards. And of course if you go back and replace a loop in the Dr Octo Rex, it will be available as an option if you need to alter the pattern playback. You don't need to re-record anything. Remember also that these blocks can be picked up, edited, shortened and lengthened as you wish, making it easy to 'paint' in backing sequences. You will notice that using this method, the eight slots are outlined in green denoting that they have been automated.

Figure 13.2
Program a sequence of REX loops by using pattern automation just like you find elsewhere in Reason.

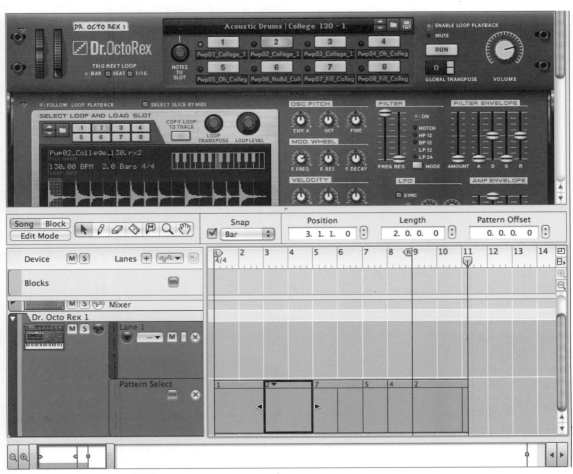

Tip

There are some great patches in the Sound Bank where all the loops in an Octo Rex belong together – that is, they contain the same kit playing intro, verse, chorus, breaks and so on. These are a good way to quickly create interesting and varied backing tracks without programming MIDI parts by hand.

Figure 13.3
Change the loop that a clip will play
back by simply clicking on it.

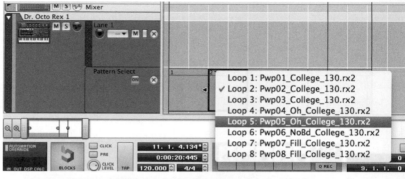

Figure 13.4
A green outline denoting Octo Rex
pattern automation.

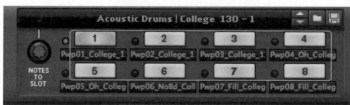

Complex beats

Another way to program pattern selection is to automate the 'Notes to Slot'
control that can be found to the left of the eight slots. Turning this will move
MIDI focus between the slots in realtime, but you can also automate it in the
usual way. Alt or option click on the knob and it is outlined in green, meaning it is automated. You will also see a new lane appear in the sequencer.
This method relies on there already being notes in the sequencer, so what
you are doing is changing the loop that those notes will be sent to. Let's say
for example that you have a Rex loop or MIDI part on the sequencer track
but you want the same pattern to play back using different loops as a song
progresses. This would be handy for keeping a sense of interest going instead
of a loop sounding too uniform. Automate the knob to redirect the notes to
different slots over time. As the track plays back, you can make it flip
between loops but using a set MIDI pattern and at any interval you like. In
theory, you could make every MIDI note flip to a new loop, making it possible to create extremely complex patterns and loops. In more everyday situations, this kind of thing is also good for throwing in alternate hits like snare
beats or sound effects from other loops but without having to create an entire
new part. One interesting trick is to map a physical controller to this knob,
allowing you to perform and capture pattern changes from a keyboard or
control surface. You can see that there are many ways to program the Dr
Octo Rex, each suited to a particular kind of performance or composition, so
why not try it out and make some great backing parts for your tracks.

Handy hints for using Dr Octo Rex

One benefit of using the more traditional Copy Loop to Track method is that
when the REX slices exist as clips on a sequencer track, you can do all the
cool stuff to them that you can do to other MIDI clips. So not only can you
double click to get inside them and start picking up, moving and otherwise

manipulating the slices to create new beats, you can use the various commands from the Tool window including Alter Notes, Extract Notes to Lanes and of course quantization, all of which can be used to modify Rex parts.

Another reason to use the Copy Loop to Track technique in some circumstances is that it also lets you route the REX clips and thus the MIDI part through the ReGroove mixer, for realtime groove quantization on the fly. As the material is in the sequencer it can be sent for processing to get a different feel while still being used in combination with the Notes to Slot automation trick to keep the sound varied.

The Dr Octo Rex opens up some interesting new creative avenues, not least the ability to make very complex-sounding electronic music with relative ease. Artists like Aphex Twin or Squarepusher pioneered the idea of cutting up beats and loops and then splicing them together using very short snippets, resulting in an insanely busy and intense burst of sound. With this new module you can achieve much the same kind of thing by automating the way the MIDI is directed to slots, or by finely editing clips together on the timeline.

In Reason 5, the old limitation with Remote has been removed. This was that you could record controllers on as many channels as you wanted, but only record notes on one track at a time. Now, when you lock MIDI controllers to different devices in the rack, they are able to record note data as well as just parameter automation. This vastly increases the usefulness of Remote as it means that several players can record a live set – notes and all – on a single computer. Dr Octo Rex is particularly useful as a live performance device.

Tip

Mapping a physical controller to an Octo Rex is a good way to flip between loops and beats in a live situation.

Tip

Consider using one Octo Rex to hold drums, another to hold guitars, a third for bass and so on. In this way you can quickly create backing tracks with variations while keeping the rack relatively clutter-free.

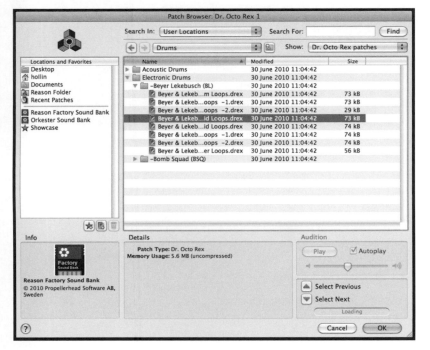

Figure 13.5
Dr Octo Rex can save patches containing up to eight different loops.

Figure 13.6
Use the editor window and the pen tool to draw in parameter changes over the course of a loop.

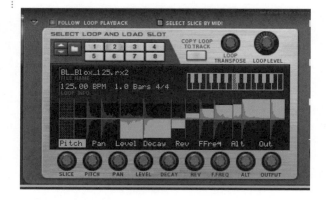

Figure 13.7
Trigger the next loop at a preset interval. For safety, choose Bar so that the current loop plays itself out.

Figure 13.8
Around the back, the Octo Rex can output individual audio slices to separate audio destinations, meaning you can process them individually.

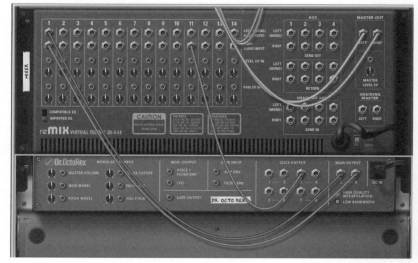

The NN-XT Sampler

The NN-XT is a bit like the NN-19, just taken a few steps further, The NN-19 is probably still the best place to quickly load up a sound and start playing. The NN-XT is where you can get more creative with your sampling. What it gives you is a host of synth-like controls for each sample you load in. In the case of a grand piano for example, this means that you can control every single sample that makes up the instrument, independently of every other sample. The rather detailed parameters of the NN-XT's Remote Editor panel are explained in the manual, but here let's look at some of the more useful tricks you can do with this sampler.

Info

In basic mode, you don't need the Remote Editor window open. The basic front panel gives you all the controls you need for simple playback of instruments.

Here is an interesting way of getting greater control over your REX loops. If you load a REX loop into an NN-XT, it will have its slices mapped over the keys of your keyboard. If you then create a Dr:Rex, load the same loop, copy its notes to the sequencer, move those notes to the NN-XT's track and delete the Dr:Rex, the NN-XT will play back the same pattern as the original REX file. Although it sounds complex this is in fact very quick and easy to achieve. The reason you may want to do it is that you will get the playback of the original loop, but with much greater control over the slices in terms of the way they are played back than you get with a Dr:Rex (Figure 14.2).

In The Remote Editor window, each sample you load is displayed down the left. In the case of multisampled instruments, this generally equates to one sample per note, and sometimes more than one velocity sample per note. Along the top is the keyboard. For each sample you can set the key range by clicking and dragging the handles of the key range, or move it as a single area by picking it up in the middle, or by using the Hi and Lo knobs. You can also drag the scrollbar at the top to navigate the whole length of the keyboard (Figure 14.3).

Figure 14.1
In basic use you can run the NN-XT from its front panel, without the Remote Editor open.

Info

The NN-XT can load NN-19 patches and REX loops as well as its own patch format.

Info

Controls on the Remote Editor panel can't be automated.

153

Figure 14.2
Copy REX notes to the sequencer from a
Dr:Rex then drag to the NN-XT with the
same loop loaded. Result? The same
playback but with greater control over
the slices.

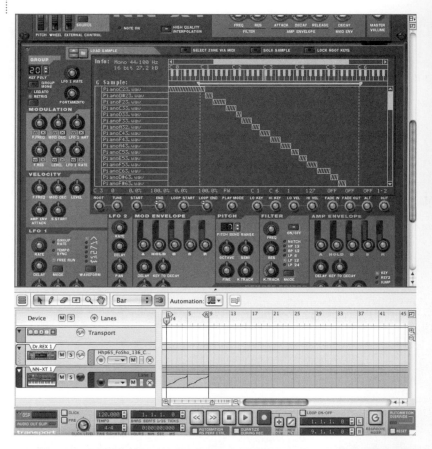

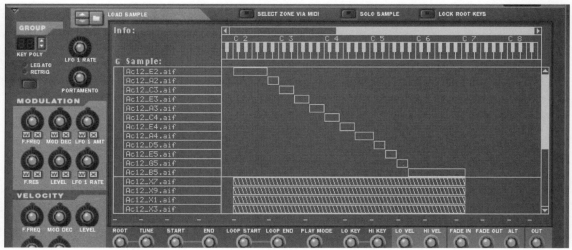

Figure 14.3
The Remote Editor shows you which
notes are mapped to which keys, and
lets you edit these settings

The NN-XT works with zones. Parameters you change for a zone affect the
sample inside that zone. Working with zones makes it easier to lay out samples over a keyboard, to layer them up and to move them around.

You can multiple select samples or zones in the Remote Editor by holding
down shift when you select them, or command–clicking (Mac) or control-

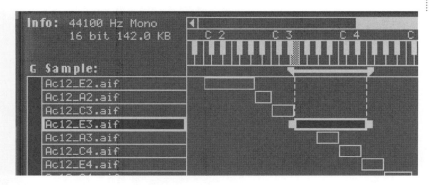

Figure 14.4
Samples are assigned to zones.

clicking (PC) on them. A quick way to load a different sample into a zone is to double-click on its name, which opens the browser window (Figure 14.5).

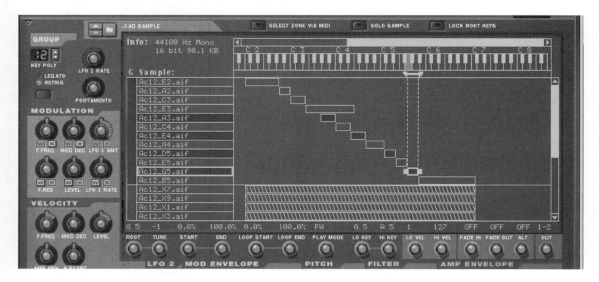

The panel of controls along the bottom of the Editor window is contextual, and changes depending on which zone you have selected at that time. However, it's easy to copy parameters between zones. Select the zones you want to copy from and select Edit > Copy Zones, or the same from the con-

Figure 14.5
Multiple select non-sequential zones to edit several properties at once.

Figure 14.6
To save time when applying the same settings to different zones, copy and paste using the contextual menu.

Info

With Reason 5's sampling capabilities, the NN-XT becomes a multisampler. Using the sample button in the Editor section, you can record in as many samples as you like and they will be placed into the grid, to be split and layered just like other instruments. Create your own sampled instruments or layer up weird and wonderful sounds to make unique creations.

Info

Any audio that you sample into a module is stored inside the project file. To edit or manage samples select the module and choose Edit > Manage Samples or go to the Tool window's Samples section.

textual menu. Then select the target zones and select Edit > Copy Parameters to Selected Zones.

To layer up several samples into one huge instrument, load all the samples into an NN-XT by using Edit > Add Zone and then simply assign every zone a key range of the whole keyboard. A single key press will now play every sample. This can create some bizarre sounds if the samples are at different speeds and pitches. You can also use the Edit > Duplicate Zone command to create variations on the same sound within an NN-XT. For example, layering up a piano with a filtered version of itself. This sort of thing can be achieved using the Combinator, but if you're just working with samples it's easier with an NN-XT.

Here's a situation you may find yourself in. Imagine you have just loaded up a group of samples that make up an electric piano. Initially, they are all assigned to the whole keyboard. Not much use. Also, they have rather unhelpful names, so manually setting them up will be a pain. There is an incredibly useful feature that can save you here. With all the samples selected in the NN-XT, choose Edit > Set Root Notes from Pitch Detection. Reason will now work out the pitch of every sample.

> **Tip**
>
> From the browser, if you multiple select a series of samples, the NN-XT will load them all in one go.

Figure 14.7
If you want to create some huge and weird instruments, layer several different samples into one NN-XT and assign them all to the whole keyboard range.

> **Tip**
>
> Like many other modules, you can audition samples by option-clicking (Mac) or alt-clicking (PC) in the sample column or the keyboard column. If you click in the sample column, you hear the sample unprocessed. If you choose the keyboard column, it plays back with any effects or changes you may have made to it.

Then, choose Edit > Automap Zones. The NN-XT will order and set the ranges of the samples based on their pitch. In practice, if you have a lot of individual key samples for an instrument, what this does is magically turn the jumble of samples into a fully working and playable instrument on your keyboard. Even after you have done this, you can still add further samples so that, for example, every time you play a certain note on an instrument, you also hear an additional effect. This could be done easily by simply having two zones with the same key range.

Figure 14.8
Reason can work out how groups of samples relate to each other by analysing their pitch.

Figure 14.9
After Reason has worked out the pitches of multiple samples, use the Automap feature to disperse them over the keyboard, creating a playable instrument. This works best with samples from the same instrument.

If you wanted to graphically separate out certain groups, you can do this by multiple selecting them and choosing Edit > Group Selected Zones. They are then placed together so they become easier to manage. There are several reasons you may want to do this. If you have layered an organ and a synth together, but want to view and edit them more easily, for example. Or, for quickly making settings to groups of zones.

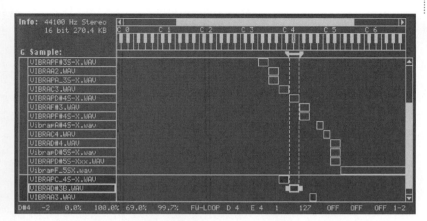

Figure 14.10
Sort samples into groups within an NN-XT to make them easier to manage

It's possible to set up velocity ranges as well as key ranges, so that different zones will play back depending on how hard or soft you play a key. This is commonly used in multisampled, expressive instruments like pianos. On a real piano, when you play the same note at different velocities you get very different sounds. To allow for this in samplers, there are often several samples for the same note, sampled at different velocities. With the addition of velocity crossfading, the overall effect is that when you play a note at different strengths, it changes just like a real instrument. With crossfading switched off, the transition between notes can be very sharp. In some situations this could be desirable, in others, not.

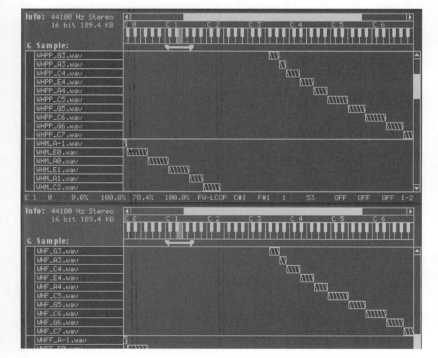

Info

Zones can be dragged up or down the list.

Tip

You could set up an NN-XT so that when you play it softly you get one instrument, but played hard it's a totally different instrument. And of course you can mix and match notes, and make settings with the Lo Vel and Hi Vel knobs.

Info

Like the NN-19, the two file browser buttons on the NN-XT load different types of sounds. The button on the front panel loads .sxt patches, and the other one loads audio samples.

Figure 14.11
In the example of this multisampled piano, there are different samples mapped to the same keys and differentiated by velocity. You can see some samples are called pp (for very soft) and at the other end, ff (for very loud).

The NN-XT has 16 audio outputs on its rear panel. These are eight stereo pairs. By default, every zone is routed to the main outputs, 1 and 2. However

Figure 14.12
Assign channels out independently for greater flexibility.

you can assign any zone to any of the eight stereo outputs by selecting the zone and using the Out knob under the Editor window to specify a channel.

You will also then have to connect those ports on the back of the sampler to something – most likely a mixer channel. You could use this to process separate zones separately from the rest of the sampler. Used within a combi, you could process the zones separately and them join them together again using a Line Mixer, then send the summed stereo output to the main mixer.

Figure 14.13
In this example, some channels are routed separately out of the NN-XT, through some effects, then submixed. The whole thing is contained within a Combinator.

It's possible to load multiple .sxt patches into a sampler at the same time! Although a single NN-XT can only load a single patch through its main interface, you can get around it by doing the following. Load two NN-XTs. Into the first one, load your patch. Then select all the zones and choose Edit > Copy Zones. Paste the zones into the second NN-XT, again using the Edit or contextual menus. Then return to the first sampler, load a new patch through the front panel, copy and paste again. Repeat until you have loaded all the .sxt patches you need. This is a quick way of combining several preset sampler patches into a single sampler. Of course you could load all the individual samples, but this is much quicker. You can route the different groups of zones to different outputs to maintain complete level control over them easily in the mixer (Figure 14.14).

Some of the functions of the NN-XT are to an extent duplicated by Reason's Remote technology and the Combinator. That is to say, creating key ranges for layered or split multi-instruments, having multiple instruments played from a sin-

Figure 14.14
Use one NN-XT just to load patches, then copy and paste the zones into a second sampler. Repeat until you have a massive multisampled instrument!

Tip

Use the Start, End and Loop controls for individual zones to tailor each sample. Choose Loop FW-SUS to sustain short sounds.

Tip

Create a sort of arpeggiator effect by looping individual samples and playing with the loop type knob.

Info

The NN-XT's LFO can be set to sync to tempo. This is really useful for creating filter sweeps for chord sounds.

Info

The NN-XT has all the usual CV ports round the back, and so can be used as a modulation source / destination for other modules.

gle MIDI key and processing separate outputs from a multi-instrument. However the functionality is in reality now doubled, as the NN-XT still retains all its features. The possibilities for combining NN-XTs into combis and then having them played by several people at once are astounding.

Here's a good way of creating a strange computerized effect with an NN-XT. Load up an acoustic piano. Now connect a Matrix sequencer to the NN-XT. Draw in some notes fairly high up the grid. A fast song tempo helps here too. Then go into curve mode on the Matrix and draw a curve. Connect the Matrix's curve CV out to the OSC Pitch in on the NN-XT. Result when you hit Run on the Matrix? A computer going mad!

Figure 14.15
Create randomized effects by connecting a Matrix to an NN-XT and entering note and curve data.

The Subtractor

The Subtractor is a real salt-of-the-earth, no-messing sort of synthesizer. For a detailed description of the principles of subtractive synthesis, as well as the history of monosynths, see the manual and the many online resources. What we're going to look at here is some tips and tricks for getting the most out of the Subtractor in everyday use.

If you're planning on programming your own sounds from scratch it's often a good idea to start with the blank patch that a new Subtractor contains by default. From there you can start to change settings to tailor your sound. The two Oscillator sections form the basis of any sound. By using both oscillators you can get a richer sound. Conversely, by using one you can get a thinner sound, if that's what you're after. For each oscillator you can choose a waveform type. These vary and by mixing and matching them you can create new types of sound. Each oscillator can also be detuned or transposed by octave, which is great for making harmonised sounds or really big sounds.

Figure 15.1
Experiment with the waveforms and oscillator controls to create new sounds.

By using the FM control on the oscillator you can create harmonic changes to the sound. By adding a lot of FM to a sound you can drastically change its timbre. Once you have selected a patch, if you click on the patch name field you are presented with a list of all patches within the subfolder you chose. So if you choose a bass sound, a list of all the other bass sounds will be shown (Figure 15.2).

Some patches – especially basses – default to a polyphony of 1. In certain cases, such as when using acid basses or lead monosynths, it can be desirable to have the synth behave in a monophonic fashion, with only one note playable at once. However, you can increase the polyphony for any sound by simply switching up the polyphony control. This is a good way of getting sound you can't create using real vintage synths. For example, playing bass chords or lead octaves.

Figure 15.2
Patches can be browsed by group from the patch name window.

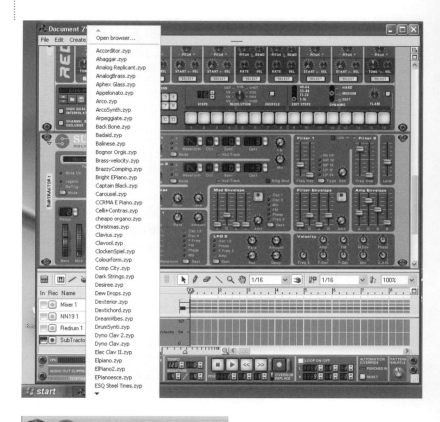

Figure 15.3
Increase polyphony to make the Subtractor play polyphonic sounds, even if they start off being monophonic.

Tip

To make synth patches sound really big – especially bass patches – try detuning one of the oscillators down an octave. To increase the prominence of lead sounds, tune it up an octave.

You can have a lot of fun with the Subtractor if you automate the controls. This is a good way of simulating the kinds of filter sweeps and hands-on real-time control you get with real synths. In Reason 3 and higher, this has particular significance because of the Remote system. By locking controllers to a Subtractor or any other synth, and creating a custom controller map if necessary, you can use the controls in realtime as you play back, even in a live situation. The more realtime controllers you have on your keyboard, the better the control you will have over the instrument.

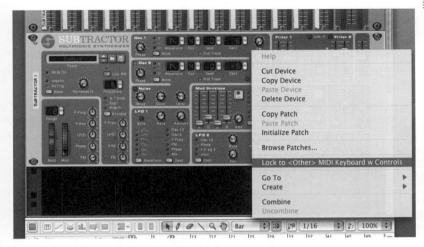

Figure 15.4
The Subtractor responds particularly
well to hands-on control using the
Remote system.

Tip

If you activate the Ring Mod
button and then play with the
mix and Phase controls for the two
oscillators you can create
interesting modifications to your
sound.

The filters on the Subtractor are different. The first is multimode and the second is low pass. By enabling the link button you ensure the sound is sent through both, and by automating the filters you can further modify your sounds.

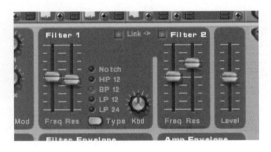

Figure 15.5

The Subtractor is meant in some ways to emulate vintage analogue synthesizers. These synths were traditionally programmed using a step sequencer of some kind. As the Subtractor doesn't have one, you can attach a Matrix sequencer to it to get the same effect. In fact this is often the best way of using a Subtractor, especially for the kinds of electronic sequences that you might want to use in your music. You can program them just using the key editor, but the results will probably sound much better if you use a Matrix (Figure 15.6).

Figure 15.6
Use a Matrix to program believable electronic loops and sequences.

Here is a good way of creating a realistic Acid bass sequence.

- Create a Subtractor and load in a bass patch. The TB Synth from the sound bank is a good start. Or you can build your own if you like.
- With the Subtractor selected, create a Matrix sequencer. It will automatically connect its note and gate CV outputs to the Subtractor's Sequencer Control inputs. A resolution of 16 steps is a good starting point for a sequence like this.
- Press Run on the Matrix and draw in some note data. Typically, acid bass sequences might contain repeated bass notes with a few variations. It's also a good idea here to drop the octave control on the Matrix so you're writing in bass notes.

Figure 15.7

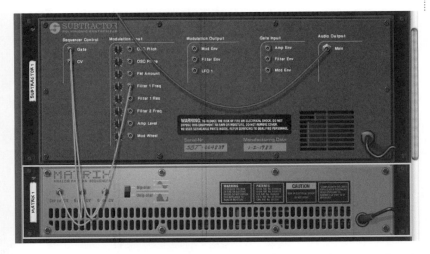

Figure 15.8

- Adjust the pattern until it sounds good to you. Now try turning on osc 2 and playing with its octave control until you get some nice harmonics going.
- Now spin the rack around and connect the Curve CV output from the Matrix to the Filter 1 Freq input on the Subtractor. Go back to the front of the Matrix and switch from Key to Curve mode. Draw in some curve data and hear how the sound takes on a much more acid sweep style (Figure 15.8).

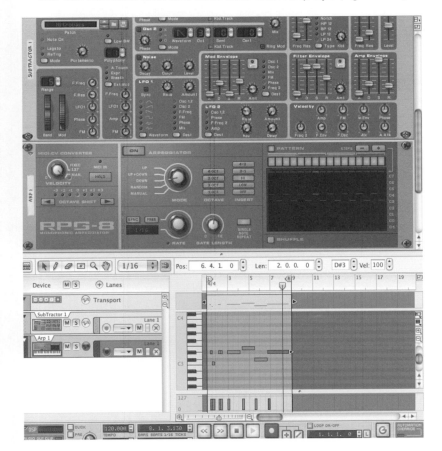

Figure 15.9
Use both curve and note data from a Matrix or an RPG-8 to modify and control a Subtractor, for great electronic loops.

- Try switching the Matrix to Bipolar mode on its rear panel. Now the curve sweep can go to greater extremes, creating an even fatter sweep effect.
- With the Matrix selected in the rack and the sequencer, choose Edit > Copy Pattern to Track, and the note data is placed in the sequencer. If you want you can now delete the Matrix and drag its notes to the Subtractor's sequencer track. However if you do this the curve control that was creating those cool sweeps will disappear. As a Matrix uses very little CPU you may as well leave it in.

The Malström

Combining granular and wavetable synthesis into a form called 'Graintable', the Malström is better suited than the Subtractor to making sharp, pulsating sounds. The basic theory is that the sounds generated by each of the two oscillators are based on graintables, which are a kind of model for generating sound. The best results often come from mixing and matching graintables in both oscillators. It's also rather good at creating sounds that morph and change over time. Here are some tips for working with the Malström.

To select a graintable (i.e. the model used to generate the sound) you can either scroll up and down using the buttons, or click on the name of the graintable and call up a list, grouped by type. You can also deactivate one or both of the oscillators to change the sound. Of course, deactivating both will produce no sound at all!

The Legato button can be used to alter the polyphony of the Malström based on the way you play. With Legato on, if you play a note and then

Figure 16.1
Browse for graintable models from either of the two name fields.

Figure 16.2
Small but important, the Legato button can alter the way the Malström responds to your playing.

Info

The Malström can be one of Reason's heavier instruments in terms of CPU usage

Figure 16.3
There are some useful controls for modifying the playback of each graintable.

another without releasing the first note, the sound will continue to progress through its envelope rather than starting a new note from the start of the envelope. This is useful if you have a sound with a long duration that changes over time. If you do release one note before you play another, the two sounds will progress independently of one another. This creates a less synced but fuller sound. For free rein, turn off Legato and manually increase or decrease the Polyphony.

Like on the Subtractor, you can use each oscillator's octave and tune controls to make significant changes to the sounds and create bigger effects. Each osc also has Motion, Shift and Index controls. These change the way in which the graintables are played back, and as such can dramatically affect the timbre of the sound. Detailed descriptions are given in the manual, but they are well worth playing around with. One effect they can have if you start to edit them is to send the sound off in different sonic directions as you hold a note.

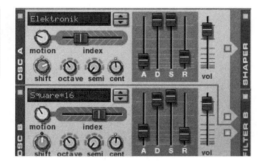

The next section that affects the sound is the Mod section. Using the curve type selector you can choose what type of modulation is applied to the sound. You can also deactivate one or both modulators. The rate knob determines the resolution at which the modulation is applied and is useful when you activate the sync button for a modulator. This puts it in sync with the song's tempo, and makes it easy to create robotic or arpeggiator effects.

Figure 16.4
The Mod sections can be synced to the project tempo for some good rhythmic sounds.

If you select one of the more unusual curve types from higher up the list, the sound will start to take on a 'chopped up' quality in sync with the project. Some good examples of this can be found if you use the patch browser to find some rhythmic Malström patches.

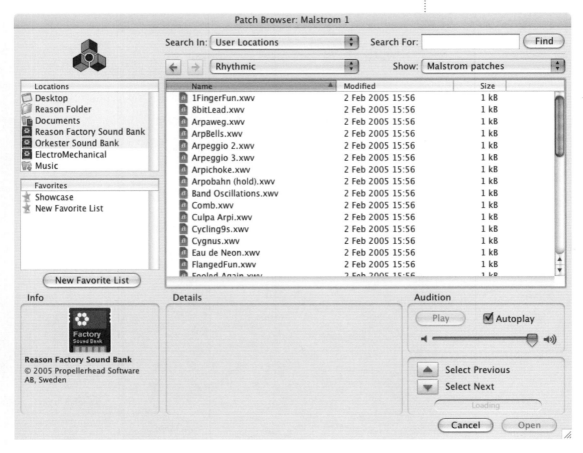

Figure 16.5

Because of the two distinct sound generators you can get sounds that appear to be made up of multiple parts. For example, locate the patch called Arpobahn. Press a key and you'll hear two parts to the sound. If you deactivate osc B you'll be left just with the thumping sound. If you reactivate osc B and switch off osc A, you're left only with the synth lead sounds. This patch also has a lot of portamento applied, which makes for interesting sweeps in pitch as you move around the keyboard.

Figure 16.6
Having two sound generation sections means you can create patches with distinctly different elements to them.

Tip

By using the tiny checkboxes you can choose to route different combinations of oscillators, shapers and filters through to the final audio outputs. Changing the way the signal is routed will often dramatically change the sound. You can route filters in parallel or in series for different results.

Info

You can create some truly weird effects by activating the invert button on the Filter Env section, and playing with the amount knob (Figure 16.7).

Around the back

The Malström has more types of connection on its rear panel than most other instruments in Reason. For example, you can bypass the filter section entirely by sending the Osc A and B audio outputs to the mixer rather than the main stereo outs.

Info

The Spread control at the bottom right of the Malström creates extra stereo width to the sound.

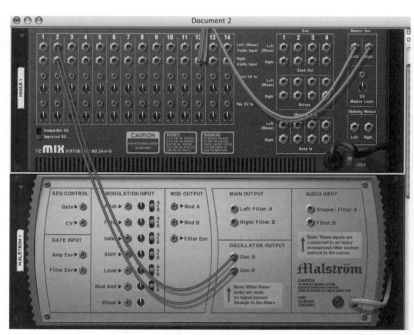

Figure 16.8
Send the Osc outputs rather than main outputs to the mixer.

The Sequencer control CV inputs lets you play the Malström from a Matrix or a ReDrum, and works best with monophonic sounds.

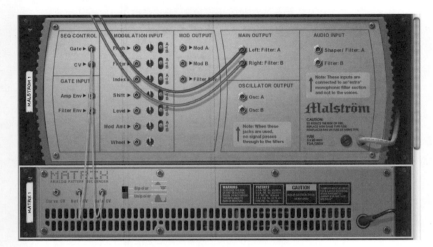

Figure 16.9
The Malström responds well to Matrix or RPG-8 control, especially for making sequences.

Interestingly there's also an audio input on the Malström. Sadly not for recording audio, but for sending external sources to the filters. If you connect an audio output from another device you can process it through the filters or shaper of the Malström. It will then be mixed with the sound being generated by the oscillators and collectively sent to the output.

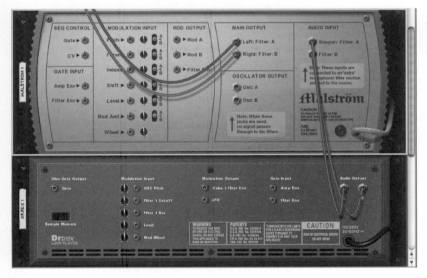

Figure 16.10
Process the audio output of any instrument through the Malström's filters.

Figure 16.11
Some interesting routing using the ins
and outs on the Malström.

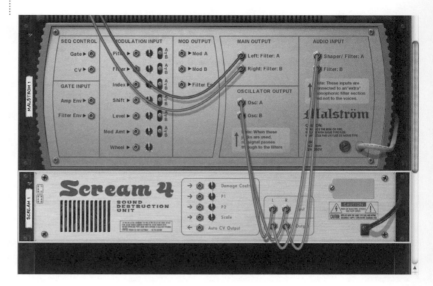

There are other interesting routing options, like the ability to place an external effect device between the oscillators and the filters on a Malström. You would connect an osc output to the input on the effect device, and the effect's output back to the audio input on the Malström.

The Thor Polysonic Synthesizer

Introduction

When creating Reason 4, Propellerhead focused much of its attention on building a brand new synth module that would bring the program back to the cutting edge of sound generation. The Thor Polysonic synthesizer was the result, and it greatly expands the palette of sounds at your disposal when making music. It's rather more complex than the other modules, but not as daunting as it may at first appear. Like everything in Reason it can be used

Figure 17.1

The Thor Polysonic Synthesizer.

in ways as simple or complicated as you wish. One thing you will probably notice about Thor is that it has a more upfront, immediate and punchy sound than Reason's other modules and as such, is likely to form the backbone of many of your compositions. Thor is semi-modular in the sense that the oscillator and filter sections can use different oscillator and filter types, and there's also a modulation bus routing section for audio and CV as well as a step sequencer and audio inputs for processing signal from other devices.

The synth and its elements

The Controller panel

By default this is what you see – a folded version of the synth, much like the Combinator's default view. It contains the key controls for patch selection and modifying certain parameters, though the really detailed stuff is hidden within the Programmer window. Here are some tips for using the Controller panel.

- The maximum polyphony of Thor is 32 voices and you can set this from the Controller panel. More voices means a heavier CPU load.
- The Keyboard Modes setting controls the way the notes react to your presses. Some modes will cancel the previous note when a new one is triggered, others will let the previous notes sustain.
- Experiment with the Portamento settings to control the amount of glide that is applied as you move between notes.
- The Note Trigger section governs whether Thor responds to regular MIDI input, input from its own step sequencer, or both.
- The two control knobs and buttons on the Controller panel are programmable and in the Modulation Routing section of the Programmer window you can assign them to practically any of Thor's controls. They can also be automated in the usual way.
- Hit the Show Programmer button to expand the programmer section and access all of Thor's controls.

The Programmer window

Like the NN-XT, this is where you make detailed settings and control the generation of your sound. It looks complicated but in reality it's only as complicated as you want to make it. It can be operated quite simply if you like. To get the real lowdown on every single parameter, check out the manual, which has some detailed explanations about the types of synthesis in use. Here are some tips for the Programmer section.

- The Voice section on the left of the programmer window contains synth parameters like filters and LFOs. It works on a 'per voice' level. The Global section on the right affects all voices.
- The Oscillator section is where sound generation begins and there are three slots available, into each of which you can put one of six types of OSC. Mixing oscillator types helps to create a more unique kind of sound.
- In the Mix section you can balance the relative levels of the oscillators you have active.

- The Filter section has three slots – two in the Voice section which work on a per-voice level, and one in the Global section which works on all active voices. Experiment with the filter types to shape your sound. The Ladder LP filter is modelled on a classic Moog filter, the State Variable filter acts as a multimode filter, the Comb filter adds pitch and phasing effects, and the Formant filter uses an X/Y grid to morph the sound into vowel-like shapes.

- You can add effects in the Global section of Thor's Programmer window, with chorus and delay available. The delay can be easily tempo sync'ed which is often a desirable effect to help sounds blend into a mix.

- The Modulation bus routing section at the bottom left of the Programmer window lets you freely route both audio and CV signals from modulation sources to destinations. Click in any column to see a list of available parameters.

- The four audio inputs on Thor's rear panel can be used to route audio in and through Thor's parameters. They can even be used for modulation – for example to modulate an oscillator's pitch with an incoming audio signal.

Figure 17.2
The Programmer window.

Figure 17.3
Modulation routing.

The Step Sequencer

The step sequencer is very useful for building short sequences or arpeggios within the synth itself. It works a bit like the ReDrum's sequencer, except it is more flexible as it controls notes and arpeggios rather than just drum hits. To activate it you need only press the Run button and select a mode – Repeat, 1 Shot or Step. It's a great way of creating quick and easy sequences without needing an RPG-8. Here are some tips for using the step sequencer in Thor.

Figure 17.4
The Step Sequencer.

The Direction switch on the left is great for creating unusual patterns. Forward and reverse are self explanatory and pendulum makes the sequence run back and forth. Random plays steps in a random order.

The Rate control sets the frequency of the playback, and the Sync button ensures it stays in sync with the project tempo. With Sync deactivated you can set a freeform rate in Hz.

For the step sequencer to take effect, the Step Seq button should be activated on the Controller panel. The 16 buttons correspond to steps. Click a button to light it and thus make the note sound. Uncheck a button to insert a rest. Use the Reset button to clear settings and the Steps knob to set the number of steps to fewer than 16.

Each knob above a step square controls a parameter as set with the Edit control in the middle. So with Note selected, each knob controls the note that step will play. With Velocity selected, the same knob controls the velocity of that note, and with Step Duration selected, the length of that step. By experimenting with these controls you can set up some great sequences quickly. The Octave control increases the possible note range for each step. This can be set independently for each step so you can have some set to a small range and others to full to create wildly varying sequences.

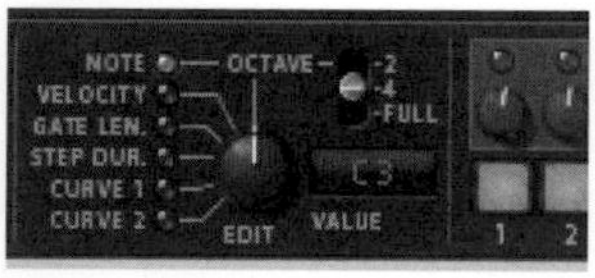

Figure 17.5
The Edit control.

Some tips for using Thor

If you open an instance of Thor you can press the Show Programmer button to expand the full control panel. It will probably have loaded a default preset or the last patch you used, so in order to program your own sound from a blank canvas, go to the Edit menu and select Initilize Patch to reset Thor. Of course there are many excellent presets but it can be more rewarding programming something from scratch for yourself.

The Programmer window of the synth is based around the idea of signal flow, so it makes sense to start at the beginning with Osc 1, which is set to Analog. In the Wave type section, try selecting the fourth wave down and you get a round tone. Now activate Osc 2 by selecting an Osc type from its dropdown menu. Try the Wavetable option as used in many classic synths like the PPG, and select a table from the list. In the Osc 1 from AM Osc 2 slider you will need to set it somewhere around the middle so that the two signals are blended together. You will also find that altering the Position knob on Osc 2 will completely change the character of the sound.

Tip

Although the basic signal path is pre-patched in Thor, you can do extensive signal routings and modulations using the Modulation Routing section. Use audio to modulate a CV signal or vice versa - Thor's modulation capabilities are virtually limitless.

Using the first filter, experiment with the different available filter types. You might find that using the Comb filter produces some interesting results if you play with the frequency and resonance controls. You may also want to activate the sending of Osc 2 to the filter as well as Osc 1, which is achieved by using the 1 and 2 buttons to the left. Next the signal passes to the Shaper section, which introduces varying levels of distortion by altering the waveform shape. There are nine modes available here, and you can control the amount of distortion applied with the Drive knob. Somewhere around the middle is often good as at the top end of the scale, sounds can become a little thin. After you have finished tweaking these controls as well as the Filter Env and Amp settings the signal passes to the Global section, which contains parameters that affect all voices currently active. Here you have the option to add a third filter through which the summed signal will pass, for even greater sound shaping possibilities. You can also add tempo sync'ed delay and chorus to fatten and add depth to the sound. Each of these has fairly detailed controls so you can be precise about the time, feedback amount, rate and dry/wet mix of the effect. For most synth noises and especially in electronic music, having the delay's tempo sync switched on is almost always desirable.

Figure 17.6
Choosing OSC types.

When using the step sequencer, repeat mode will be the most useful as it loops round and round so that you can build up a sequence. The Direction switch lets you set the direction of the sequence. Forward is the most common but you can achieve interesting effects by choosing pendulum or random. The sequencer's controls are quite minimal to look at but there is a real depth of features cleverly hidden behind the Edit knob. The red squares under each of the 16 steps are note on / off indicators and the dial above each one controls whatever parameter is currently selected on the Edit knob.

Figure 17.7
Choosing filter types.

Thor features a highly flexible modulating routing section, where you can use signal from any part of the synth to control other parts. This makes for some interesting modulation possibilities. For example, In the source column, try choosing something that you know is generating signal, like Osc 1 and in the Destination column, choose something that you know is available to be modulated such as Filter 1's frequency. You will need to raise the Amount slider by clicking and dragging it but you will hear that the one signal now modulates the other. The more complex a patch, the more available sources and destinations there will be for creating weird and wonderful sounds. Often you get unexpected but great sounding results by patching parameters to each other in this way. Remember that you can set the Amount slider to negative values as well and that the more modulation slots you use, the more unique the results you can achieve.

There are four assignable controls on Thor's front panel which can be freely assigned using the modulation matrix, a lot like the system used in the Combinator. Select a button or rotary control as the source and then any parameter as the destination, such as Chorus dry / wet amount, for example. Then set the amount slider to determine the amount that the control will affect the destination parameter, 100 being the maximum. Then you can click on the name field on the assignable controls and name them according to their new functions.

Figure 17.8
Setting up effects within Thor.

Figure 17.9
Setting a rotary control to modify effect levels in the Modulation Matrix.

One particularly interesting use of this new and massive sounding synth is to incorporate multiple instances of it into Combinator patches and then split and layer different sounds to create some really stunning results which also sound great played live. Although geared towards electronic sounds, Thor is just as capable of atmospherics and cinematic effects as acid squelches and bleeps, so there is something here for everyone.

Tip

If you're feeling lost for inspiration when programming Thor's step sequencer, use the Edit menu or right click on the module and choose Random Sequencer Pattern. Repeat as many times as you like until you get something that works for you.

Tip

Thor can receive audio input from other modules in the rack which it can process through its filters or use as a modulation source for triggering many of its own parameters. It also has four audio outputs so you can route signal on from Thor to anywhere else such as effects, a line mixer or a Spider audio module.

Figure 17.10
Multiple instances of Thor in a Combi for a massive sound.

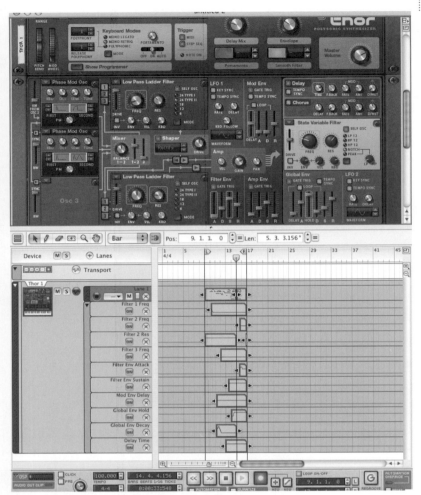

Figure 17.11
Automating Thor's controls using sequencer note lanes.

The effect devices

Effect devices don't generate sound, they modify it. Part of Reason's flexibility lies in the fact that as well as having multi-functional instruments and a sequencer, it also has many different types of effect device to colour your sounds and add depth to them. It's fairly essential to use effects of some kind on your tracks. They all have very different uses but the most common are reverb, delay, compression and distortion. There are a couple of things to say about the general use of effects. The first is that if you're making more conventional music, less is often more when it comes to effects. Using them sparingly can often be a lot more effective than applying them in great swathes. Conversely, if you are being more experimental, over-using effects can be a great way to get some really unique sounds. Here are some common features of all the effect devices in Reason.

Effect devices are created in the same way as instruments, by selecting Edit > Create or right-clicking in the rack and choosing a device. They can also be deleted in the same way as instruments. They are patched using cables, and can be renamed by clicking their name field to make it editable.

Tip

When an effect has signal playing through it, the LED meter on its left will light up. You can bypass or mute an effect without actually deleting it by using the control on the top left corner.

Tip

If you have edited (i.e. moved) knobs on an effect device you can quickly reset them to their default position by command-clicking (Mac) or control-clicking (PC) on them.

Figure 18.1
Create effect devices from the Create menu or the contextual menu or by dragging from the Tool window.

183

Figure 18.2
An example of a complex effect module built inside a Combinator. This can be saved and loaded very quickly.

Different effects all impose varying amounts of drain on your CPU. The smaller effects like the Phaser or RV7 reverb create relatively little strain. Some of the RV7000 or MClass patches by comparison are pretty heavy.

Effects can be freely routed just like instruments. With the Combinator you can create complex effects chains within a Combi and then save it as a combi patch. Then when you need it again, just call up the single patch rather than re-building it all from scratch. This can save a huge amount of time copying and pasting or using template files.

Most of the parameters on effects units can be controlled in realtime. With the Remote system this means that you can map individual controllers to, say, effect type selectors, depth amounts or delay resolutions, and change them while you play. This can give your music a much more organic feel. To achieve the same thing in a studio setting, they can of course be automated in the usual way. Effect automation can be recorded on multiple tracks at once as of Reason 4 and higher.

Insert or Send?

Effects are applied in one of two ways – inserts or sends. To create a send effect, select a main mixer (ReMix), a chained mixer or a smaller line mixer and then create the effect. It will automatically be routed as a send effect

Figure 18.3
Using Remote to control a Reverb unit in realtime from the keyboard.

through the mixer's aux bus. To create an insert effect, select any instrument module in the rack and create the effect. Wiring is then automatically done so that the instrument's outputs are routed through the effect and then on to the mixer. You can create any number of insert effects as a chain attached to an instrument, or as many as your computer can handle, at least.

When effects are used as inserts, a signal chain is in force. That is, the signal is passed through the effects in a hierarchical way, top to bottom (unless you manually rewire them). With sends, you determine how much of the 'wet' (effected) signal is mixed with the 'dry' signal.

Info

Some of the effect devices have CV (Control Voltage) inputs which can be used creatively to receive CV signal from instruments to modulate their output in unusual ways.

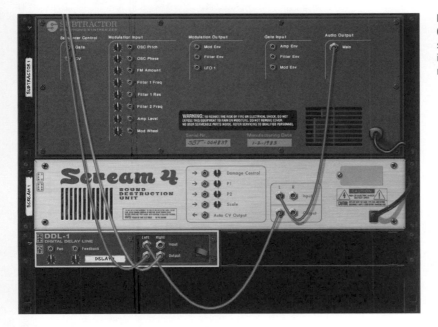

Figure 18.4
Create an effect whilst an instrument is selected and the effect is applied as an insert, between the instrument and the mixer.

Which effect to choose?

The kinds of effects you might use on most channels – say, reverb, compression and delay, are best to attach to the mixer as sends. If every channel needs a little reverb, rather than attaching a reverb unit to each instrument at great cost to your CPU, attach one to the mixer as a send and then

Figure 18.5
Some effects attached to the main mixer as sends.

just send differing amounts of each channel to it using the aux sends on the mixer. You will only be able to use one preset on the reverb unit, but there's nothing to stop you using more than one of the same type of effect as a send (Figure 18.6).

Figure 18.6
Frequently used effects work best attached to the mixer as sends.

Creating chains of insert effects is a great way of messing with a sound before it even gets to the mixer. By using the Combinator to do this, chains are easier to manage and also can be stored as Combi patches for instant recall.

When you use inserts, the order of the effects units changes the sound. For example, if you have a distortion, then an EQ, then a reverb you will get a certain sound. If you move a device or add another one into the chain

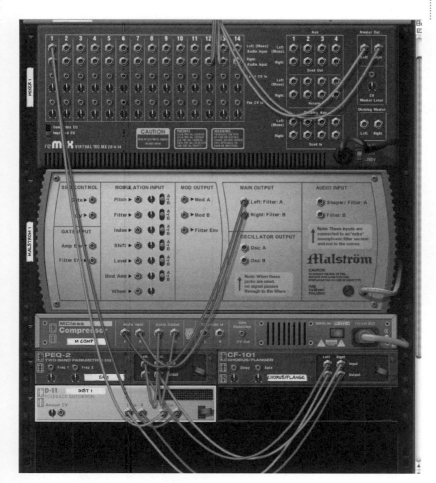

Figure 18.7
By creating a chain of inserts on an instrument you can build unique effects.

Tip

There's not much point using an effect as a send if you're only planning on sending one or two instruments through it. In that case, better to use inserts.

somewhere you may find the behaviour of devices further along the chain changes as they process the different sound. For example, if you apply an EQ that takes out the high frequencies of a sound, the delay that comes next in the chain may suddenly become much less pronounced. These sorts of changes are very specific to the kinds of sounds and effects you work with, so it's hard to come up with any definite rules. One thing that is for sure is that by combining effects in chains you can create unique sounds that you can't get with any one single effect.

Scream 4

The Scream 4 is much more than just a distortion unit. It lets you add all kinds of warmth, crunch or overdrive to your sounds. One side effect of using digital music sequencers is that the signal they produce can sound overly clean and lacking in bite. Almost every type of sound – synths, basses, drums, pads – can benefit from some warming up using a Scream 4. Unlike most of the other effects units it can store and load its own patches, with the suffix .SM4. This makes it easy to save and recall your favourite Scream effects. Here are some tips for using the Scream 4.

Figure 18.8

The Damage section has ten basic types of distortion available, and each has two controls which alter different parameters depending on the type of damage you choose. There are no hard rules about what type to use for what – in fact the most interesting results can come when you're trying things that you may not at first think will work. However, the ten types of effect do have certain real-world counterparts.

- Overdrive is typical of the sound produced by analogue amps when they're pushed right to the limit. Used subtly it adds 'edge' to sounds without making them jump out of the mix.
- Distortion is a bit more in-your-face than Overdrive, and better for heavier crunch effects.
- Fuzz is more of an angry, 1960s guitar type of effect.
- Tube distortion is warmer and more dense than other types.
- Tape is an interesting one because it recreates the kind of artefacting typical of magnetic tape saturation. Used properly it can make sound much more lifelike and less digital-sounding. It can be a good idea to apply this to the entire mix, by inserting it between the mixer and the hardware interface.
- Feedback feeds your sound back into itself, producing some strange results.
- Modulate blends the signal with a compressed, filtered version of itself, resulting in resonant distortion effects.
- Warp is particularly nasty and produces a high, mangled sound.
- Digital emulates the low bit resolutions of early digital equipment. Bit reduction is a particularly unique kind of digital sound. The lower the resolution and rate, the more chopped-up the sound. Great for vintage arcade game types of effect.
- Scream adds a bandpass filter before the distortion stage. Use the two control knobs to control its frequency. By moving the P2 knob you can get some good wah-wah effects.

Figure 18.9

The Cut section can be used to fine tune the effect, boosting or cutting the lo, mid and hi frequency bands.

The Body section simulates types of acoustic space in which your sound is effected. Some presets correspond to a type of speaker cabinet and others are unique to the Scream 4. By experimenting with these settings you can further tweak your sound.

One of the Scream 4's more hidden features is its CV controls. On the rear panel are four CV ins and one CV out. By connecting CV outs from instruments to these inputs you can control the amount of damage effect, the two

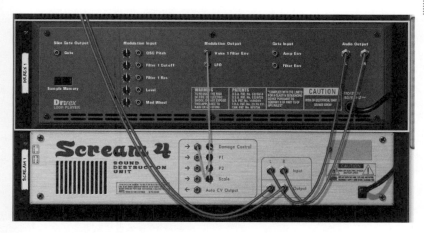

Figure 18.10

P knobs and the Scale parameter. Here is an example. Create a Dr.Rex player and load a drum loop. Then connect a Scream 4 to it. Go to the rear panel and connect the Mod Output from the Dr.Rex to the Damage Control input on the Scream 4. The result is a much more chopped-up drum sound with much harder attack.

Try switching the cable to the LFO output on the Dr.Rex. The effect is a kind of reverse drum loop.

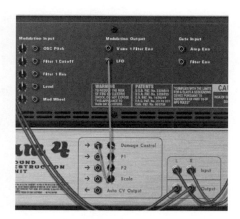

Figure 18.11

In another example, create a ReDrum and play a drum loop into the sequencer. Attach a Scream 4 as an insert and route the Auto CV output from the Scream 4 to the Pitch CV in on one of the active drum channels. The pitch of that drum hit is now actively modulated by the Scream 4. There are more uses for the Auto CV out. For example, by sending Auto CV through a Spider unit and inverting the signal you can achieve 'ducking' effects, whereby increasing the volume of one sound source will decrease the volume of the other.

For modules that have individual outputs for each of their channels like the ReDrum or NN-XT, it's quite possible to process only specific channels through the Scream 4, or any other effect module. Simply manually patch the relevant channel through the effect. In this way you could for example process the snare and bass sounds through an effect, but leave the cymbals

Figure 18.12
Modulate individual drum channels using the Scream 4.

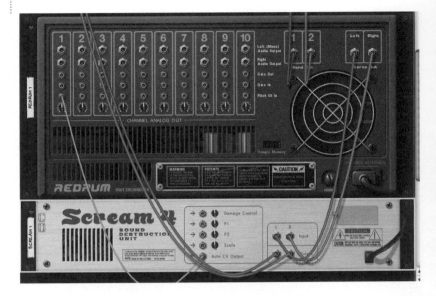

Figure 18.13
In this example, several drum channels are sent to a Spider audio merger, then through the Scream 4, then grouped and sent to the mixer. The remaining drum channels go straight to the mixer as usual.

clean and running to the mixer. In this situation, using the Spider Audio merger / splitter is useful (Figure 18.13)

As the Scream 4 has different sections, you can activate only the ones you want. For example, by only using the Body section you can create specific sonic effects related to the quality of a sound without applying any distortion at all. To create wah-wah effects, connect an instrument's LFO CV out to the Scale CV in on the Scream 4 and play with the controls until you get the effect you want.

RV7000

Reverb is one of those curious effects that, if it does its job properly, you shouldn't notice unless it's turned off. What reverb does is effectively make things sound further away, so it should be used with care, unless that's the effect you're particularly going for. A good trick is to use a very small amount of short reverb on most channels. Although you can use a reverb as a send effect and apply a little to each channel in the mixer, remember too that software allows you to insert as many as you want throughout the rack. Different types of reverb work better with different sounds. Strings, for example, benefit from lush, warm reverbs. Drums sound good through short, snappy reverbs.

Figure 18.14
The RV7000's remote programmer allows detailed reverb editing.

The RV7000 has a good selection of presets, and like the Scream 4 it can store and load patches. To get into more detailed editing of the reverb, open the Remote Programmer by clicking on the socket to the bottom left of the unit. Now, by using the three buttons on the left of the programmer you can access the three types of parameter – reverb, EQ and gate.

In the Reverb section of the programmer, use the eight knobs to control all the parameters of the reverb. The most useful are Algorithm, which switches between basic reverb types, Tempo Sync (where applicable) and Diffusion. The Dry / Wet control on the main panel controls the overall amount of effect applied. You can get some really cool dub-style delay effects by using the reverse, multi tap, echo and spring algorithms. For more cinematic reverbs, try the FilmScore preset. Remember that you can chain these units together to create multi-layered effects.

By using the EQ controls on the RV7000 you can shape the character of

> **Tip**
>
> The Gate section lets you create gated reverbs, triggered either by audio, MIDI or CV. All the controls on the RV7000 can be automated, so you can create some mad reverb changes as your songs play.

Figure 18.15
Create effects chains of reverbs with varied dry / wet amounts to create that perfect effect.

the reverb, not the original sound. If you are mixing wet and dry versions of the same sound you may need to drop out certain frequency bands in the wet signal.

Additional effects units

The smaller effects modules are more straightforward and very simple to operate. Here are a few tips for using them.

- The RV-7 reverb is a good alternative to the RV7000 if CPU power is a problem. Interesting presets include Stereo Echoes and Low Density.
- The DDL-1 delay can be set to delay in different units. Switch between them to get different styles of delay. In Steps mode the delay will always sync to tempo. In MS mode, the delay operates freely.

Figure 18.16

- The D-11 Distortion is a no-frills alternative to the Scream 4.
- The ECF-42 filter can be used as a regular filter but you can also route CV or MIDI from a program device or the sequencer to create pattern-controlled filter effects.
- The CF-101 unit adds chorus or flanging to a sound, and can be used to create richer textures.
- The PF-90 phaser adds sweeping effects, ideal for guitar and vocal sounds.
- The UN-16 Unison works by adding a sort of chorus, and gives the effect of a wider, fuller sound.
- The COMP-01 compressor evens out the loudest and softest parts of a sound, increasing the overall volume. Basses and drums particularly benefit from compression. Use heavier compression for a 'pumped' effect.
- The PEQ-2 lets you precisely boost or cut frequencies in the sound that is processed through it.
- The Spider Audio Merger / Splitter can either take several audio signals and merge them into a single output, or take a single source and split it up to four ways. There are several uses for this. You could for example use it to sub-group a number of modules. Or, by splitting, you could send one signal through several effects units and into separate mixer channels, which saves time and power by ensuring you don't have to start duplicating devices or sequencer tracks.
- The Spider CV Merger / Splitter can either merge four CV sources into one, or split one into four. You could for example use one Matrix device to control several instruments, or have several instruments modulating a single unit.

Figure 18.17
Use the Spider to merge or split audio for many different purposes.

The MClass effects

The MClass suite of mastering effects helps to bring a more professional sound to your Reason tracks by adding various processing modules to the signal chain. Good mastering gives music greater depth, punch and clarity, as well as ensuring a good overall level of gain. Like mixing, it depends on the track, the monitors you listen to it on, your ears and the room you listen in. There is a lot of good information available out there on how to master, but let's look at a few of the MClass's tricks.

The MClass effects are available separately or as a combi, and can be applied individually to any instrument, and used as many times in a rack as your CPU can handle. When you are using an MClass Combi for mastering, attach it between the mixer and the Hardware Interface. This will ensure that

Figure 18.18
A Mastering combi sits well at the very final audio output stage of Reason.

Figure 18.19
The Factory Sound Bank has some good mastering combi patches to get you started.

the whole signal passes through it. Make sure you select the Hardware Interface and then create the Combi.

A Combi is the best way of using the MClass effects specifically for mastering. Click on the name field and you can select from a list of presets with sensible names like Dance, Hard Rock and so on. Don't be afraid to try a preset that you may expect not to suit your music. It could be that the Drum and Bass preset works really well on an acoustic track – you never know until you try.

You can tweak any of the presets, or build your own mastering combi by creating a Combinator and filling it with any of the effect modules. You can of course mix the MClass and other effects to get unique sounding effects chains.

The MClass effects are equally adept when used individually, as insert or send effects. Here is a look at what they do.

MClass Equalizer

The has two bands and high and low shelving bands. You can use the Lo Cut switch as a sort of 'rumble reducer', as it removes all frequencies below 30HZ. EQ can help to make sounds sit properly in the mix and blend together. It may be that you EQ a guitar, for example, to sit well in a mix. It doesn't matter that by itself it might sound thin, as long as it works in the track. If you are using your own samples you may need to roll off some of the top end, if any of them have hiss recorded on them.

Figure 18.20
Use the Lo Cut switch as a sort of 'rumble reducer'.

MClass Stereo Imager

The MClass Stereo Imager addresses one of the more long-standing issues with Reason's mixdowns – the lack of real stereo width. Splitting the signal into Lo and Hi frequency bands, you can widen out the higher frequencies whilst narrowing the lower ones. The result of this is that the top end gets opened out while the bottom end is pulled in and made tighter. You can process the separate bands separately by manually re-patching on the rear panel.

Figure 18.21
The MClass Stereo Imager improves stereo width.

MClass Compressor

The MClass Compressor features a Soft Knee mode to give you a more gentle compression and reduce the undesirable 'pumping' effect that can result from harsh compression. It also has sidechain inputs, which allow you to use an audio signal to trigger the compressor. You can use this to create the so-called 'ducking' effect, whereby when one sound plays it will dramatically reduce the volume of another.

Figure 18.22
The MClass Compressor features a Soft Knee mode to give you a more gentle compression.

MClass Maximizer

The MClass Maximizer tackles the problem of quiet mixes by limiting. It increases the overall perceived loudness of a mix without ever distorting or clipping. Use a combination of Soft Clipping and boosting the output gain to make a mix louder without it sounding too pumped or hitting the red. This can be particularly useful to use as an insert if you have imported your own samples into a sampler and they are too quiet. Rather than pushing faders to the max, use a Maximizer.

The use of mastering effects is a very personal process. Some people prefer less, some more. But what is true is that they make quite a difference to the overall sound quality of your mixes. To see just how much, try switching them off and hear the life and energy instantly drop out of your track.

Tip

There's nothing to stop you using more than one Mastering Combi in a rack. However, be careful not to overdo it and apply too much effect, which can leave your track sounding over-produced.

Figure 18.23
The Maximizer increases overall perceived volume.

BV512 Vocoder

Vocoding is a fairly familiar effect these days – the process of taking a sound and making it robotic, or synth-like. Some of the interesting uses for the vocoder involve moving away from the more obvious applications and instead vocoding other sounds like drums or guitars for special effects. Here are a couple of things to remember about the Vocoder.

It's a little more complex than the other effects, in that it requires two types of input to work. A carrier signal (typically a pad or string patch) and a modulator signal (typically speech or vocals). The Vocoder looks at the fre-

Figure 18.24
The BV512 Vocoder is a little more
complex than the other effects.

quency characteristics of the modulator signal and applies them to the carrier, outputting the result. Essentially, the speech is 'playing' the synth. The speech sample isn't being effected as such, but rather its characteristics are being used to modulate another sound. The reason it works best with pads or strings is that they have a constant quality to them. You can use any sound, but with sounds that are already rhythmic, the effect of the vocoding is much less apparent.

As Reason doesn't record audio directly in, you can't sing straight through a Vocoder. Instead, use the NN-19, ReDrum, REX or NN-XT modules to load pre-recorded samples that you have created in another program. One of the advantages of loading lots of samples into, say, a ReDrum is that you can have them all running through a single Vocoder, which will save you power and space in the rack.

The more filter bands you use on a Vocoder, the more accurately the output will match the characteristics of the modulator signal. By using the Band control you can toggle between band settings. The setting you use will depend on your desired effect, as a more lo-fi effect can be achieved by using fewer bands. Alternatively, if you select the FFT setting you will get the most accurate voice vocoding setting. This essentially simulates 512 frequency bands, hence the name of the module. It's best to use FFT for vocoding vocals, not instruments.

Figure 18.25
Choose a Band setting that suits the type of effect you need.

A full guide to setting up the Vocoder can be found in the manual. However, here are some useful tips for using it in day-to-day situations, and some possible applications for it.

- Carrier devices should ideally be bright, synth or string-like patches. This is because the more signal there is, the more the Vocoder has to play with and so the better the eventual output. They also tend to sustain indefinitely rather than tailing off, which is helpful in this case.

- A Subtractor or Malström can be used as a carrier with the just the Init patch loaded. Make a few tweaks to the detune knobs, and off you go.
- If you assign MIDI to the Vocoder's sequencer channel (assuming you have created one) you can 'play' the individual bands using MIDI keys.
- The band level controls on the Vocoder can be automated, with a separate subtrack for each band. You must have first created a sequencer track for the Vocoder before any automation can take place.

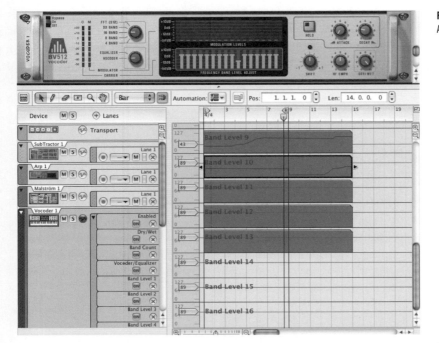

Figure 18.26
Automating the bands on a vocoder.

- By using a rhythmic loop – say, a REX drum loop – as the modulator source, you can effectively arpeggiate the carrier signal. Basically this means that when you play, whatever is loaded into the carrier module plays rhythmically based on the sound of the REX loop. If you duplicate the Dr. Rex player in the rack, you can have synths and drum loops playing the same rhythm, which sounds great.
- To get a more precise rhythmic modulation you can of course program your own beats in a ReDrum and use that as a modulator signal.

The Vocoder has comprehensive CV in and out on the rear panel, which means you can get very creative with using it both as a source and a destination for modulating other devices, or using others to modulate individual bands. They can also be cross-patched if you're feeling really adventurous.

You can use a single device both as a carrier and a modulator, with interesting results. Use a Spider Audio splitter to send audio from a device to both sets of inputs on the Vocoder. If you do, it's worth adding an EQ or a distortion module between the Spider and the Vocoder to give it a bit more punch. This works well with drums, giving a heavily filtered effect.

Tip

When creating a device to be a modulator, hold down the shift key. This will stop it from routing to the mixer, saving you a step when you then patch it to the Vocoder's modulator input.

Tip

Using the Remote Override Edit mode or Keyboard Control mode you can automate the switch that toggles between vocoder and EQ mode on the Vocoder. You could punch between the two on the fly.

Figure 18.27
Using a Spider to creatively modulate signal through a vocoder.

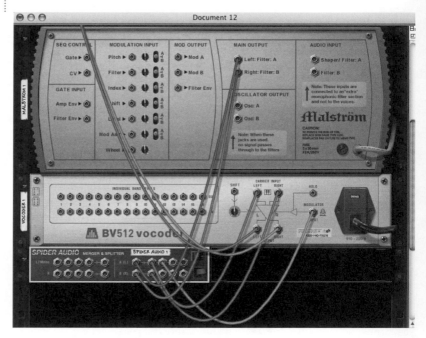

The Hold button will freeze the current state of the Vocoder and the sound won't change until you click it again. This is good for playing live as it gives you more control over how the sound plays. Again, the button can be controlled from a MIDI keyboard using Remote or Keyboard Control modes, leaving you free from the mouse to concentrate on playing.

Figure 18.28
Freeze the state of the vocoder with the Hold button.

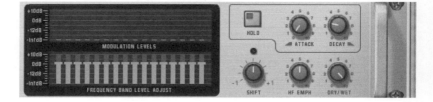

The RPG-8 Arpeggiator

For a program containing synthesizers and used extensively in the production of electronic music, it was odd that Reason lacked a dedicated arpeggiator module. True, the Matrix sequencer does a passable job of triggering sequences, but it was a workaround rather than a full solution. Reason 4 introduces the RPG-8 Arpeggiator. Like the Matrix it generates data rather than sound until you connect it to a sound module or synth. Unlike the Matrix, it requires you to play notes through it rather than drawing them into a grid. Like a classic arpeggiator the RPG-8 is monophonic which means that it can only play a single note at once, though there are creative ways to achieve polyphony by using mutiple modules. It's able to receive MIDI input directly from a keyboard or other device, or from notes drawn into its sequencer note track. With the RPG-8 selected and connected to a module capable of creating sound you will find that any notes you play will be repeat-

Figure 18.29
The RPG-8 Arpeggiator.

ed in staccato fashion based on the settings on the arpeggiator. It acts essentially like a MIDI effect in Cubase or other sequencer by processing the MIDI input in realtime and altering it before it reaches the sound module. As such it can also alter any MIDI data dragged onto its track, meaning you don't necessarily have to play it in live through the arpeggiator.

A quick tour

The RPG-8's On button must be activated if it is to process sound, be it live playing from a MIDI keyboard or data from an existing sequencer track. It must be connected to a sound source such as a synth. The central section of the module controls the type of arpeggiation that will be applied to the notes. The Mode, Octave and Insert knobs control the direction, octave jump and preset repeat of notes respectively. You can change the rate of arpeggiation by using the Rate knob. With Sync selected, it syncs to the project tempo. If you select Free, you can manually set the rate in Hz which is interesting but more suited to experimental than conventional music. The Gate Length knob governs the length of arpeggiated notes. The longest setting is Tie, where two notes run together.

Figure 18.30
The control section.

The Pattern section displays the current pattern. When this section is switched off, the RPG-8 will arpeggiate any data played through it based on the settings in the control section and display the currently held notes in the pattern display. If the MIDI Hold button on the left is activated, it will keep repeating the pattern indefinitely. If set to off, it will play only as long as you hold the keys down. In this mode, the RPG-8 can display as many notes as you are holding down. If that's more than 16, it will continue beyond its 16 steps to display any remaining notes.

If you activate the pattern section, you can use up to 16 steps by clicking the squares so they light up. Now, pressing a single note on the keyboard will cause the RPG-8 to automatically create patterns based on the settings in the control section, using the note you pressed as a root note. If you hold a chord, it will play the notes making up the chord in a sequence determined by the settings you have made with the Mode, Octave and Insert controls. In

Figure 18.31
A simple Arpeggiator pattern.

a very simple example, holding a chord of C with settings of Up, 1 Oct and Off, it will play the notes of C, E and G in a repeating pattern.

In a more complex example, a more complex chord is held with some mure unusual settings on the RPG-8 including the Shuffle switched on and reading from the ReGroove Mixer's Global Shuffle settings to add groove and variation into the pattern, making it less mechanical. Certain steps have also been switched off to make thE pattern a little more interesting.

Figure 18.32
A more complex pattern.

If you record onto the sequencer track for an RPG-8, the notes are recorded as regular notes and continue to be processed through the Arpeggiator. That way, the pattern remains editable. However if you want to render the notes down to a track in order to copy or edit them in greater detail, do the

Figure 18.33
Rendering an arpeggiated pattern to the sequencer and dragging it to the sequencer track of the device it is triggering.

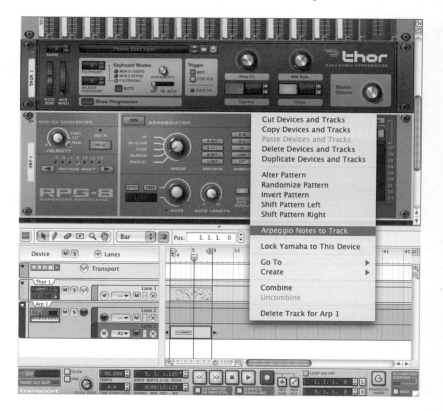

following. Right click on the RPG-8 or go to the Edit menu and choose Arpeggio Notes To Track. The arpeggiated pattern – which you will see is far more complex than the original notes – will be placed into a new sequencer lane on the RPG-8's sequencer track. These can then be editied or copied like any other sequencer data. It's worth dragging the notes onto the sequencer track of the device being controlled (say, a synth) and muting the RPG-8. Otherwise, you will get two lots of the same pattern trying to play at once.

Some tips for using the RPG-8

If you open a project you can try connecting an RPG-8 to a Subtractor with a bass patch loaded, or something similar. Arpeggiator effects work much better with short sounds as they tail off in time for the next one to start. Try setting up a loop and making sure the On button is activated, record a riff using the default settings. Ensure that the Arp 1 sequencer track is selected so the arpeggiator is active. The initial Rate setting of 1/16 may be a little fast unless the tempo of the project is quite low. If it is, try switching it down to something lower using the Rate knob. It makes a lot of sense in most cases to leave the Sync button activated as it will seamlessly mesh the sequence and your project tempo. You may need to quantize the recorded notes if your playing was slightly out since playing through the RPG-8 can initially make judging timing tricky. The default Octave setting is 1 which will keep the notes simple but you can experiment with settings of 2, 3 or 4 octaves which will cause the notes to jump up one or more octaves in sequence. Another useful setting to play around with is the Gate Length knob which governs the length of each note. Turn it towards zero to make each note shorter and sharper, or towards Tie to make each one longer. Turned all the way to the right, the arpeggiator is effectively muted as only the original notes are played, with no arpeggiation.

Once you have made a sequence in the conventional way, rendered and moved it to a sound module, you can then return to the RPG-8, create a new pattern for the same module, render it down and go on making new patterns by building up different note events on the sound module's sequencer track. By the same token, you can copy and paste data between two arpeggiators or simply duplicate one and attach it to another device. In this way you can back up a sequence by using another sound to play an identical sequence – a great way of reinforcing it. In fact if you right click on a module you can choose 'Duplicate Devices and Tracks', reconnect the new modules to each other and then go on to edit the sound used by the duplicated sound mod-ule and if you wish, the pattern played by its arpeggiator. One interesting trick is where for example you have a sequence playing to a 1/16 resolution, to duplicate it and use a more subtle sound in the sound module, then set the Rate on the duplicated arpeggiator to 1/8. Playing the new pattern at competing for space with the original.

Arpeggiators aren't only useful for electronic music, though they are found extensively in it, but also for subtle uses in other styles. As well as sim-ply altering notes they can be used as sources to modulate all kinds of other parameters through CV outputs. Most importantly, they enable you to create patterns and sequences too complex to input by hand or with the mouse.

The Matrix Pattern Sequencer still exists in Reason so you can still use it for everything you did before. The RPG-8 is however much more adept at traditional arpeggiator tasks like creating repeated note patterns with easily switchable up / down and rate settings. The Matrix remains a quick way to draw data curves to control CV in other modules.

With single held notes, the Mode setting has no effect as the module doesn't have to interpret more than one note at a time. To make it more interesting, with one sound module and RPG-8 already in place, try creating a second sound module and another RPG-8. This time, choose a new sound. When you record some notes over the first loop, try holding down a couple of chords or at least several notes. The arpeggiator will interpret them and play them in sequence based on its settings. By default the notes will go up but try playing with the Mode setting, using Down, Up/Down and Random to change the pattern. Also alter the Rate setting for further customisation. By default the module will play every note of a sequence but you can change this by clicking on the Pattern button to the right and then clicking on any of the red buttons when you want a note not to sound. This is how you insert rests into a sequence. If you decide you want to shift the notes up or down an octave, this is done using the Octave Shift buttons on the left up to three octaves in either direction.

Figure 18.34
Automating an RPG-8.

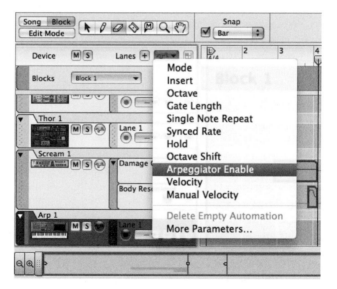

Try dragging or copying data from other sequencer tracks into the sequencer track for an RPG-8 to make it run through the arpeggiator. Remember to mute the original track or you'll hear both the 'clean' and arpeggiated versions.

Most parameters for the RPG-8 can be automated in the usual way by activating the relevant automation parameter and drawing in values. In the case off on / off parameters these values are either 0% or 100%.

The RPG-8 has CV in as well as CV out ports and these can be used to control Gate Length, Velocity, Rate and Octave Shift.

Figure 18.35
The RPG-8's rear panel.

The RPG-8 can be used as a modulation source, generating stepped modulation sync'ed to tempo and controlled by note input. It can also be used as a MIDI to CV converter.

Exporting from Reason

So you've spent ages on building and automating your tracks, and now it's time to export them so you can put them on CD and play them to the world. There are two ways in which you can do this – by recording the track to a realtime media like a CD recorder, DAT or MiniDisc, or by exporting it to an audio file. The latter is by far the most common with Reason, but here's a quick description of how you might do it using the first method.

Exporting in realtime

This used to be the accepted way of mixing down before computers became so commonplace. Basically it just means playing the track out in realtime and recording it to some kind of magnetic or optical media like a tape or CD. It is a perfectly acceptable way of mixing down, although in reality, now that every computer has a CD burner, and you're more likely to want to upload mp3s of your work, it often makes sense to export straight to the computer's hard drive. One case in which you would almost certainly need to record out to DAT or CD in realtime is if you have routed Reason's tracks out directly through your audio interface by manually patching channels through the Hardware Interface. In this situation you may well be processing Reason's

Figure 19.1
If you are routing audio from Reason out through your soundcard's separate outputs and mixing on an external hardware mixer, realtime mixdown may well be the way to go.

tracks through external hardware effects and a mixer, and those effects would only be recorded if the total summed output of Reason (main stereo outs plus any separated channels) were all collected together and recorded on a single device.

Mixdown is a good time to apply a fade in or fade out to your track. This is done by automating the master fader. As you record, move the fader smoothly up or down. Alternatively, open the automation subtrack for the master fader by alt or control-clicking on it. Then draw automation in with the pen tool or, better still, with the line tool to create a smooth ramp. In Reason 4 or 5, create a track for the mixer and use the pen tool to draw in a ramp. Remember that to automate anything on the mixer you must first create a sequencer track for it. The master fader will gain a green outline once automated.

Figure 19.2
Automate the master fader for a smooth fade out.

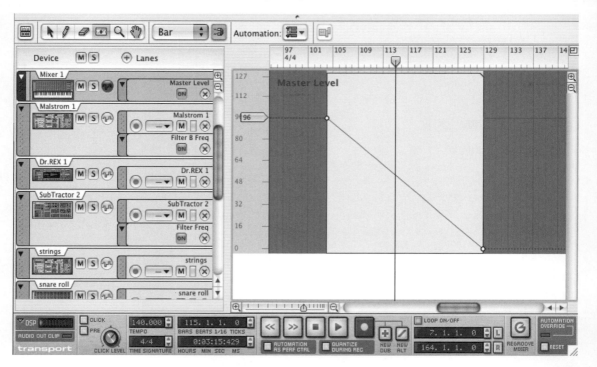

A note about ReWire

If you are running Reason in ReWire mode with SONAR, Cubase, Logic or any other compatible program, Reason's audio outs are inextricably linked with that program. The export options in Reason will be greyed out as they can't operate independently of the host program. In this case, selecting audio mixdown in the host program will include Reason's output in its mixdown, meaning you don't have to worry about it.

Figure 19.3
In ReWire mode, Reason's export options
are transferred to the host program,
such as Cubase.

Checking everything

There are some tips for actually mixing your music in the chapter on the Mixer, which all apply here. After you have perfected the levels and the automation for your track, make sure the left and right markers are positioned over the start and finish of your track. Leave at least one bar of empty space either side. If your track ends with an echoing sound of any kind, make sure to leave a few bars of space, or it will be cut off. If you need more space on the timeline, drag the E marker further to the right.

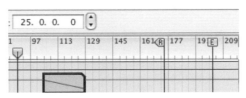

Figure 19.4
If you need more space, drag the End
marker to the right.

> **Tip**
>
> Zoom out so you can see your entire track graphically on the timeline. This will help you check if the markers are in the right place.

Make sure everything that should be unmuted is unmuted. Select File > Export Song as Audio File. Choose somewhere sensible to put it. If you're on a Mac, choose the AIFF format. On a PC, choose WAVE. For audio CD you'll usually want to select a sample rate of 44.1kHz and a bit depth of 16 bit.

As a rule of thumb, don't go above or below these settings unless you know why you need to. Most video editing programs run at 48KHz but can happily deal with audio sampled at 44.1. If you are exporting to 16 bits you can tick the Dither box, which will make sure there's no distortion introduced by changing bit depths. Reason now renders down your track, including all the effects and automation, to a single file. If the track is long and has lots of effects and instruments, this might take a moment or two.

Figure 19.5
Choose an audio output format depending on your platform of choice.

Figure 19.6
The Dither option ensures clean bit rate conversion.

If for some reason you need every track as an individual file, for remixing purposes, you can simply solo up one track at a time and export it. This is a bit time-intensive, and is better achieved by using ReWire to record tracks simultaneously through into a host sequencer, if you have the software.

If you haven't already inserted one, it's a good idea to put an MClass mastering Combi between the mixer and the Hardware Interface and select or modify a preset that suits your music best. The changes to the sound introduced by the MClass effects are included in the mixdown. You'll be surprised by how much bigger and wider it can make your track sound.

Figure 19.7
Introduce a mastering combi between the Mixer and the Hardware Interface to improve the overall sound of a mix≥

There are some other export options worth mentioning.

- Export MIDI File will export the entire track as a MIDI file, ideal for sharing over the internet or for backing up.

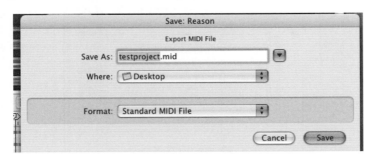

Figure 19.8

- Export Device Patch will export the current patch of whichever device you have selected. This is really just another way of performing the save function from the front of the modules.
- Export REX as MIDI File will create a file containing just the MIDI data contained in a REX loop, not the audio.
- Export Loop as Audio File is especially useful if you are taking small sections of music into other programs to work with. For instance, if you have a great drum loop, you probably only need four bars of it to take into Pro Tools to do a remix. Or, for multimedia purposes where small loops are necessary for quick download speeds, taking a bit of something is easier than taking it all. Remember when you do any kind of export from Reason that what gets exported is what's audible. That is, if you don't want certain tracks to be present in the exported audio file, you have to mute them. Anything that's muted will be left out.

If you are working on different machines, remember that you must have the same sets of sounds present on all machines for projects to play back properly. You can use the Search and Proceed warning box that pops up to find the files, but only if they're on the system somewhere. If you are using lots of your own samples and moving around it's a good idea to use the ReFill Packer that comes with Reason to organize them into ReFills, which are easy to manage.

Tip

If you are ReWiring through to another DAW, or using Record, you should be able to use the host DAW's Batch Export features to output any Reason channels being streamed through automatically to separate audio files.

Sharing and publishing

If you choose to upload your songs to the web or send them to anyone, there are steps you can take to ensure your work is identified as your own. Here are some tips for publishing songs.

If you choose File > Song Self-Contain Settings, you can see exactly what parts of what ReFills you are using in your track. This window displays audio files, not patches. Remember that Reason project files are just instructions – they don't include any external audio data, although in Reason 5 they will contain any audio that you have sampled in yourself. For this reason, you

Figure 19.9
Use the supplied ReFill packer to organize and share your samples and patches in ReFill format.

Figure 19.10

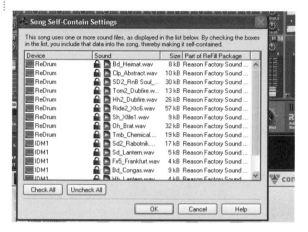

have to make sure that if you are sending someone the file as a Reason project rather than an mp3, you must also include any relevant ReFills. Otherwise, when they open it they will just be prompted to locate the missing files. Projects will still open, but any missing files will be replaced by silence. Self-recorded audio samples should be included.

By selecting File > Song Information you can embed data about yourself and your music. You can select a 256x256 pixel image, enter your URL and email and some text of you like. If you choose to show the Splash window on open, it will always pop up when the song is loaded (Figure 19.11).

Regular Reason project files can be modified by whoever opens them.

Figure 19.11
Embed text, URL and email information and your choice of picture in your song file.

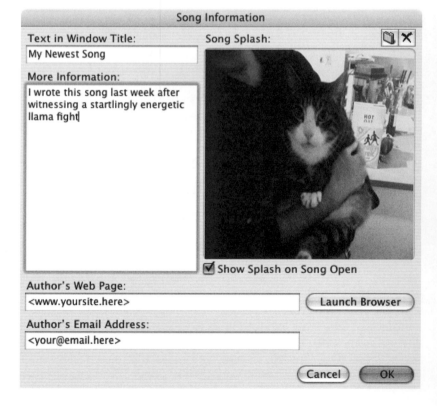

However, if you don't want anyone to be able to mess with your work, choose File > Publish Song. What you then create is an .rps file which can be opened and edited but not saved. Also, if the song is edited in any way, it cannot be exported as audio until it has been quit and re-opened in its original form. This means that it's impossible (or at least very hard) for anyone to remix your track or change it without your permission. Interestingly, the option to

Figure 19.12
A published Reason song is relatively well protected against changes or borrowing of patches.

Tip

Any audio that you sample into a project in Reason 5 is stored internally, so you don't have to worry about where it lives. This also means that a project with lots of samples can be quite large. Samples loaded from outsie of Reason remain separate and must be included manually.

export patches is also greyed out in .rps files, meaning that if you have created a killer synth sound, nobody can steal it – unless you want them to!

Info

In the Song Self-Contain window you can now see samples you have recorded, and choose to manually tick or untick them to make them a part of the song file or not. Samples from the Sound Bank are included because Reason assumes the banks will be present, and samples from third party ReFills must also be included if you want to send the project file to anyone to work on.

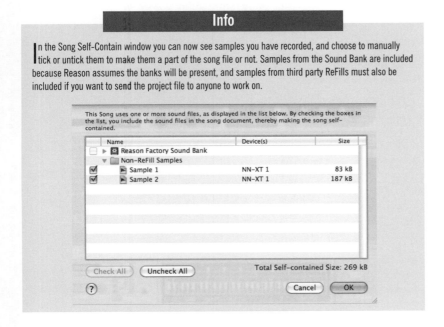

On the whole there are no cross-platform issues between Reason on a PC or Mac. A Reason file is just a Reason file, and that's that. As there are no plugins to deal with, that's not a problem either. The only possible incompatibility is if you have some external audio files on one system but not another. Be aware also that you can't open files made in a newer version of Reason in an older version of the software. If you are working in version 5, stick with it. If you're working in version 3, don't start working in version 4 unless you are prepared to switch permanently.

Index